INSPIRE Me, Ms. America!

A Journey to Wellness con SABOR

INSPIRE Me, Ms. America!

A Journey to Wellness con SABOR

DOLORES NEIRA

Cover Design: 99 Designs
Editing: Kimberly Nash-Amezcua

TABLE OF CONTENTS

A FLIGHT TO MAUI LIKE NO OTHER

"Let Your Hopes, Not Your Hurts Shape Your Life."
– Robert Schuller

A message comes over the speaker above my head saying, "It is now safe to remove your seatbelt" and before you know it, we're off! As a small business owner, Corporate Consultant and Licensed Brain Health Trainer, I receive requests from various organizations throughout the nation to provide training programs that will help their teams improve focus, increase productivity, and create a harmonious workplace. Therefore I travel frequently.

I used to dread flying so severely that I would have to see a doctor prior to the scheduled flight to request a prescription for the "patch", a slow-release chemical band-aid of sorts that would act as Dramamine and would relax me into a semi-drowsy state throughout the flight. Later in my career, someone helped me with that phobia by simply sharing this one logical statement, *"Once they close the plane doors, how much control do we really have, so we might as well make the best of it."* *#TRUTH.*

Since then, somehow my brain has shifted its focus to a challenge rather than a feeling of fear which used to cause anxiety throughout the entire flight.

Flying high, at 36,000 feet, I am surrounded by hundreds of total strangers, who are equally trusting in the law of gravity, so I play a game called "Race-against-the-clock" and the writing frenzy begins.

Thoughts of Charles Schultz's character, Schroeder a piano playing genesis, from the comic strip "Peanuts", come to mind. I pound away at my laptop as he does his mini-grand piano while performing classical music from artists like Beethoven. Never once does he look up to pay notice to Lucy, a friend who is enamored with him, gazing, head in her hands, with hearts shooting from her eyes, and seemingly, madly in love.

The airplane lifts off and it's as if a timer has started for me and I frantically attempt to hammer out yet another chapter addressing the gigantic topic of mental wellness, brain health, and how the two correlate when connected to the onset of Type 2 Diabetes, (T2D). My goal during this plane ride has been laid out for me very clearly prior to accepting this trip to Maui. My urgency is to find the "magic formula" for those who are suffering from the repercussions of uncontrolled Type 2 Diabetes.

To be clear, in this book, I will be focusing solely on Type 2 Diabetes, not Type 1, as that is an entirely different beast. I seek to find just the right message to spark hope in the person who reads it, and to inspire them not to give up. And, in turn, I hope the information prepared will serve as a vehicle to save someone's "life and limb", literally.

Writing this book took a lot of self-introspection, positive self-talk, and confidence-building. I wrestled with this self-defeating thought, *"So you're diabetic and you want to help, but you can't because you're **still** diabetic"*. Each time I would get a twinge of inspiration, to put pen to paper, I'd find myself pausing and allowing many negative thoughts to penetrate my mind. It was "imposter syndrome" or that feeling you get when you start to question your expertise on any particular subject and I let it take me down, many times throughout this process of over six years, to be exact. At present, so many more loved ones, within my extended family, have succumbed to the disease with horrific outcomes. Fewer limbs, mental health problems related to obesity, and even deaths. So, I said, "Not anymore, I am ready!" I will no longer stand by and watch when something I can say or do might potentially impact and change the course of someone's life for the better.

Upfront and honest, I am not a medical doctor. I am speaking out for those who can't and for those who have struggled with not knowing what to say when they see their physician. I have taken it upon myself to research medications, secure tools, and locate resources that are on the market and try them on myself, yes, on myself. I am my own true guinea pig and over the years, I have seen failure and success.

That said, this book will share evidence-based practices used by myself and others to manage Type 2 Diabetes, T2D. It has become a personal passion of mine to step in and challenge the status quo of mediocre intervention techniques and lack of information for those most affected by this disease, namely the poor, marginalized, and low-income who continue to show the highest number of new cases. With the highest rising numbers in Black and Latino communities in America. In short, *"INSPIRE Me, Ms. America! A Journey to Wellness con SABOR"* will be my legacy. My message to the readers is simple, we've got to start talking about this silent killer so that others can avoid the ills of this chronic disease and can live a life of health and wellness as they were intended to live.

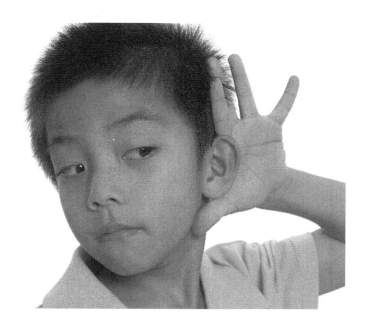

WILL THEY LISTEN?

To push back on the "imposter syndrome" I began by doing research and plenty of it. I read everything that I could get my hands on. I documented everything and kept three years of spiral notebooks full of stats and data. I knew I needed concrete person-to-person interviews and a deeper dive into investigative inquiry to answer the "why".

Next, I set up a series of "Think Tanks" or meetings with interested people. These Think Tanks were offered throughout the state of California and within the Nation as well. I worked with colleagues and other work associates who were willing to help launch this effort. I offered dinner in-kind at a local healthy(ish) restaurant and used the time to ask the hard questions. They were all aware of the purpose for the meeting beforehand, so the topic was not a surprise. We were ready to enter into a serious discussion about real-life cases. Many of the participants were struggling with the condition themselves.

Here's the harsh reality:

> Insulin is a hormone that allows you to process sugar and is secreted by your pancreas. Your cells need insulin to take glucose from your blood and use it for energy. Too much insulin released too often can make your body less sensitive to it -- a condition called insulin resistance which can lead to Type 2 Diabetes. Once awakened, you must take an active role in putting it back to sleep before it becomes more difficult to manage. If left unmanaged, it will result in continual high blood sugar. Consistently high blood sugar can lead to heart disease, kidney disease, stroke, neuropathy, and blindness.

I traveled throughout the United States namely, California, Texas, Hawaii, and Washington. My approach was enthusiastic and high energy as I was certain that everyone wanted/needed to hear this information, unfortunately, that was not the case.

Although the participants were supportive, the topic was a bit heavy, and honestly, who wants to talk about a disease? Before I realized how hiding from it would negatively alter my life, I didn't want to talk about it either!

With the Think Tank participants, I wanted to talk about a cure or a way to effectively manage the disease; maybe life hacks or success stories.

I love family, whether it's the one we were born into or the one that we choose throughout our lives, I call them "FRAMILY", (Friends + Family). And to watch them suffer, truly tormented me. My mother passed due to Diabetic complications, and four of my five siblings suffer from the disease. Everyone in my immediate family struggles with obesity, which is a known precursor to T2D, not a guarantee but a real indicator of future health complications. I justified not talking about it because the truth was just too raw and too uncomfortable for many. I mean, I was being respectful by not talking about it, right? I thought to myself, "I'll just try and manage my diabetes, then be reminded of my progress or lack thereof, once a year at my annual doctor's appointment, then feel bad for a brief time, and then go on about my business, and live my life". Months passed and a slew of diabetic-related events continued to occur in my family, I was devastated!

IT HITS HOME

One by one loved ones in my immediate circle began seeing health-related complications, eye surgery to repair burst blood vessels due to the T2D complications, a diagnosis of pre-diabetes for a loved one in their 20s, a toe amputation, a leg amputation and then a distant family member's mother passed away with no legs due to multiple amputations.

One morning, I woke up startled. I think I may have been praying in my spirit and thought to myself, "That's it! No more!" It was 4:00am in the morning and I got up and walked to my home office, picked up my marker pens and giant Post-it flip chart paper, which I used primarily for training workshops, and began mapping out the chapters, one by one. I didn't stop until noon. I remember my husband looking in on me and inquiring if I was okay and if I wanted lunch. I responded, "No thanks and please leave me alone, I am in the ZONE ". This time, my internal voice was saying, "I know stuff!" and "If I get stuff wrong, I'll have to correct it, but the stuff that I know to be right can potentially save a life."

I challenged myself and thought, I know that T2D can be managed, controlled and even reversed, so I wrote that on my paper, I know that there is a brain-gut connection and that what we eat triggers our brain to react negatively. I know that sugar is a legalized drug that creates addicts and obesity. And I know and will know much more in time.

I submitted to that task of writing this book and committed to what I believe is a journey of mine, designed by God, for my life's purpose. Sharing the news that Type 2 Diabetes is reversible, not completely erasable, but reversible and that we can have an optimal life that is healthy and well, is my story.

ANGELS ON EARTH

Time management was the new dilemma. I had been working consistently and had little time to devote to writing but instead of putting the book project away, I'd wake up at 4:00 am and work until 6:30 am three mornings a week. Then the call from one of my angels on Earth, Sandy, came in. She had always been my muse, of sorts. Whenever I'd get stuck in my career, she'd somehow show up, out of the blue, with a new book or other resource, a true inspirational goddess. I answered the phone with a surprised expression, and heard, "Hey Friend, would you like to go with me to Hawaii and meet some of my colleagues?" asked Sandy. She came in just when I needed her most. My immediate response was, "I wish, but I honestly can't afford it and have no time". She continued by offering a free bed in her hotel and the desire to "bless" me with free meals for dinner. She said, "All you have to do is pay for your flight". Needless to say, two weeks later, I found myself boarding a Hawaiian Airlines flight to Maui. I was in awe with how this all fell into place. First the offer of a free bed, then when ordering my ticket, using my credit card, the customer service representative mentioned that I had enough points to have it taken care of completely! And finally, a request for Board Retreat Training from a local non-profit presented itself, unexpectedly. The problem was they were not able to pay me. I never turn down working with nonprofits even when they have limited or no funds. I took the work and to my surprise, was given a VISA gift card as a thank you for my services. It ended up being just enough to cover my expenses! It was a God-given gift and I received it as a sign to get away and get focused and to finally write this book. "How does that even happen?"

After the five-hour plane ride, while listening to the sounds of Hawaiian music, I had it! This book had been in my thoughts for so many years and now it was ready to be born. The outline was organized and written before landing in paradise and I used the remainder of the time to map out: *INSPIRE Me, Ms. America! A Journey to Wellness con SABOR.*

I dedicate it to my mama and to all those who suffer from T2D and Brain Health issues brought on by elevated blood sugar levels.

For that week in Maui, I cleared my mind of any negative thoughts, released, and forgave those who caused me ill will, and began writing with a single goal; to help someone else by first helping myself. I am on my journey to health and wellness and may not be there yet, but I am much better off than I was yesterday! I have used my memoirs to share the life of a Mexican American Female who is in the process of reversing Type 2 Diabetes and can still eat food that is tasty and true to her Ethnic identity. I share this information with a sense of urgency, though, as Latinos hold the highest percentage of reported cases of Type 2 Diabetes, followed by Black Americans and third, Asian Americans. My story is true. Developing it was held hostage in my heart and mind for many years and I now know that I must share it. That said, I say to myself, "ADELANTE Dolores, (Onward and upward) Ms. America!

o n e

EATING LIKE A GABACHO!

"Be grateful to anyone who has ever loved you or tried to love you."
I've Been Thinking – **Maria Schriver**

AMIGAS PARA SIEMPRE - FOREVER FRIENDS

I am grateful for challenges, and because of them, I believe that I have become a stronger, and more resilient person. Do I embrace the turmoil, NO, but one thing is for sure, in everything there is a season and a lesson to be learned, if, and only if you stop and look for it.

I have a friend, who I am convinced came into my life for one purpose. I am not saying for a season, but more for a particular purpose.

For me, years before I would get to have the life that I do in the present day, my amiga - who I will refer to from this point forward as Chill, was predestined to be there as a guide, and an angel on Earth. This lovely lady helped me to transition out of an abusive relationship with a high school boyfriend and into my destiny. She was my bridge into the next phase of my life.

Our friendship has been able to withstand the test of time; fifty-three years and counting, at the time of this entry. Like many friends, we drift in and out of each other's lives and call or text for special occasions where we pick up right where we left off. Nevertheless, I remain forever grateful to her. She was the sixth of seven siblings. Chill had a shy demeanor until she had something seriously important to say, then her assertiveness would surface and you'd see an entirely different personality. She was extremely intelligent and had older sisters who challenged her solely because they were accomplished in academia as Master's candidates. Chill was a tall, caramel-colored Latina, with long straight jet-black hair and a big smile. Her bright white straight teeth were what was most pronounced about her face, followed by her big dark eyes that would squint when she laughed or felt embarrassed. She was modest and rejected the many compliments she'd received regarding her beauty. She could have easily been mistaken for a woman of Hawaiian heritage and was a very proud Mexican American female with strong cultural knowledge about her family and their past generations. She taught me much about what it meant to be Mexican-American.

We were introduced, for the first time, by her eldest sister, Anna. Anna was studying Sociology at San Jose State University. Anna's Master's thesis project involved the study of inner-city youth. Her task was to choose a group, then study their environment, identify a problem, and invest time and effort into effecting positive, long-term change. Simple task, right? Anna chose to begin a Girl Scout Troop at Tierra Nuestra (Our Land) apartments in East San Jose, CA. and it was there that we met. Chill was not her real name, but I met her as such and have called her that to this day.

For many, starting a Girl Scout Troop might sound easy enough, but not for those who lived in this particular apartment building. The Master's Thesis study would involve the recruitment of young girls, 10-14 years of age, to support the Girl Scout traditions to honor God, Country, and the Girl Scout promise which is to live by the Girl Scout Law of Sisterhood.

Anna began the Girl Scout troop in an apartment complex that was primarily used as emergency and low-income housing. Many of the tenants were coming from homeless situations, or recent financial hardships of some sort. It was considered to be a high crime area, known for violence and drug trafficking. Tierra Nuestra was a tough place to live, race riots, and gunshot sounds were commonplace. For my family and I, it was a place to start over again as my mama was evicted from her PAID-OFF home due to being behind on her property taxes. I was personally glad to be out of La Casa Blanca. Our home was foreclosed on, and we were sent to live at Tierra Nuestra. We had no choice in the matter and were forced to leave our home and move into this housing project many referred to as the "ghetto". Even though her alcohol addiction was a deterrent to a productive life for the family, my mother managed to shelter me from the evils of life as best she could and to instill in me a love for education. Being a product of the 50s and 60s, during the Civil Rights Movement, my mother was always ready to fight the "MAN" and to stand up for justice and equality. I remember her drilling into my psyche the following phase and saying, "Education is our Freedom, Mija and you should never forget that!" Later on in my high school days, I would go on to win a contest for Cinco de Mayo Queen using that same topic and chant that my mother taught me. Anna arrived and began the recruitment for the Girl Scout troop members and for some reason, she focused on me.

Anna would often drag along her little sister Chill to the Girl Scouts meetings. "Hello, are you Anna's sister?" I eagerly inquired. She looked down at me with a glare. I was ten-and-a-half at the time and had not even reached 5 feet tall, and Chill was very much taller. "Yes", she responded with a tone of frustration. Chill never really wanted to be involved with the Scouts, you see by 11 years of age she was already 5 '9 and had a fully developed body so the pressure was on her to be "cool" and act older and more mature than she really was; frankly, she was popular, and I was not. I compare the relationship to that of "Smalls" and "Benny the Jet Rodriguez" in the popular movie about baseball, *The Sandlot*. Little did I know how much that brief introduction with Chill would affect the course of my life. After a while, the development of our true friendship would be postponed until high school, 9th grade to be exact. It turns out, Chill was able to persuade her big sister Anna that Girl Scouts were simply "not for her".

TOGETHER AGAIN

Early on in our lives, we shared many milestones. First, high school graduation. Then, leaving home and going away for college, and eventually becoming roommates. Chill was there when I met my now husband and was even my Maid of Honor at my wedding over 40 years ago! We were kindred spirits, for sure. After the birth of my first child,

Chill and I were adamant about our desire to lose weight and to get back into our high school dress size. After both graduating with our Master's degrees, hers in Counseling and mine in Education, we both decided to move back to our hometown. She had become a guidance counselor at a local middle school while I was a college admissions coordinator. Once the baby arrived, I became a stay-at-home mom, desperately trying to understand all the new life changes that accompany the most important role I would ever be privileged to have; motherhood. Motherhood was a lifestyle shift from seriously selfish to consistently selfless. I learned quickly that even though those two words looked and sounded alike, they were completely different behaviors, as far as the East is to the West.

A CULTURAL CONFLICT BETWEEN HEALTH AND HAPPINESS

We always supported each other's desire to look and feel better. On one of our many attempts to get fit, I remember we joined a weight loss program in which you pay for predetermined frozen meals for a set of introductory weeks and included weekly management meetings. At these meetings, a representative would weigh us in and report the weight to our counselor. That was the ultimate in peer pressure and accountability. On this particular day, I contacted Chill so we could coordinate our plans for arriving at the meeting together. "Do you want me to come by for you or do you want to meet there?" I asked. "No, please come to my home and we can walk from here," she said. I recall reminding her to eat light so we could show good weight loss that morning.

I arrived at the front door and was greeted warmly by Mrs. Alvarez. A beautiful, full-figured lady with salt and pepper hair and big round eyes covered by glasses that made them look even bigger. Standing no taller than 5'1, she was Mexican American with fair skin and light caramel-colored eyes. She was wearing a "muumuu" dress with a vintage purple and white floral apron and was busily preparing the Saturday family breakfast. Mrs. Alvarez was a welcoming soul who embraced and recognized me as part of her "adopted" family as she did many other strays. At the time, Chill and I had been friends for almost 16 years, so she was like a second mother to me. Entering her house, the scent of delicious *Mexican breakfast foods hit my face. Fried papas, (potatoes), home-made flour tortillas, chorizo, (Mexican spiced sausage), fried eggs, salsa de molcajete (hand-ground in a mortar and pestle) and coffee, complete with a splash of canela, (cinnamon), and Mexican hot chocolate. This breakfast could be described as decadent and even celebratory for most but for this family, and many Latino families, it was the weekly Saturday morning brunch. A meal that was often a way for families to gather before the weekend got underway. Honestly, Bobby Flay, the culinary chef known for his Southwest cooking would probably not be able to match this meal as most of the time, it was made with "Mama's" love.

MEXICAN INSPIRED BBQ SALAD

Eagerly anticipating my weigh-in, Chill came to the door and asked if I could wait just a few minutes longer as she went to gather her shoes. I responded, "No problem", but dreaded being invited into her home because I knew that once inside the temptation to have "just a bite" would quadruple in intensity. Anyone who has ever been on diet-after-yoyo-diet knows that forcing strange and unfamiliar foods into your body in a quest to lose weight is not sustainable. Just as I feared, Mrs. Alvarez asked "Dolores, so nice to see you, are you hungry?" I thought to myself, "NOOOOOOOOO, don't do it!!! You're going to weigh in!" I politely responded, "No thank you, Mrs. Alvarez, I have already eaten." Refusing an offer of food, from a respected adult, especially one who is a mother figure, in Mexican culture can be very risky. I proceeded to say a quick prayer under my breath and thought to myself, "Oh no, I hope I didn't offend her?" Just as she was about to respond to my rejection of food - delicious, flavorful, dripping with luscious goodness- food, Chill interjected. The exchange of words that ensued in that moment became the premise for this book. I remember it as if it were yesterday. What Mrs. Alvarez shared next was a valid concern and one of the primary reasons that individuals reject adopting health and wellness habits and prefer to live life in the moment. It is the reason that diets don't work but lifestyle changes do.

"Mom, what are you doing!? Chill asked while speaking in a tone of aggravation. "I'm cooking Mija, what does it look like to you?" Mrs. Alvarez responded. She had recently been under a doctor's care for some health-related issues due to the stress from the recent passing of her husband of 45 years. This morning, Chill witnessed her mother scooping handfuls of Manteca brand lard into a tall black cast iron pot in preparation for the refried beans that she would serve for Saturday breakfast that morning. Chill just stood there in frustration, wide-eyed and open-mouthed. "Mija, are you hungry?" Knowing that we were on our way out, she continued to say, "Take a burrito for you and your amiga". She encouraged us to eat as she tried to ignore her daughter's judgmental stares. I felt a feeling of embarrassment come over me, not so much for me but for the fact that there was conflict brewing between the two of them. Chill proceeded to say, "Mom, you know the doctor said that you have to eat differently, or you'll get worse." She proceeded to invite her mom to our weight loss program meeting and offered to pay the weekly dues. With a frustrated look on her face, Chill motioned for me to move toward the door so we could leave for our weigh-in. The last comment we heard from Mrs. Alvarez that day was in "Spanglish" (English and Spanish words mixed into a sentence), communication delivery. She yelled over the sounds of sizzling pinto beans being dropped into a pot of hot, bubbly lard, "No thank you Mija, you go on to your meeting and eat the food that Gabachos, (white people), eat. That food has no sabor, (flavor), I would rather eat what I like and die happy than to be sad while eating your tasteless food." Walking out of the house, I glanced at Chill and noticed a sad look on her face. We both proceeded on to our weight loss meeting and after the dreaded weigh-in, discovered that we both had lost a couple of pounds each. We then agreed that it was not nearly enough weight loss to warrant all of the sacrifice and effort we had made throughout the week. We walked from the meeting location to Chill's house where I had parked my car. In silence, both Chill and I were in deep thought as we felt the dilemma between what we knew to be healthy behaviors and the cost of abandoning our cultural ideology that is attached to our culinary ethnic choices. Choices that were not as healthy as what we were being taught but that we did not want to give up. We never spoke about it again.

LIFE IMPACTING MOMENTS

We're all familiar with the acronym YOLO, (You Only Live Once). Or, how about FOMO, (Fear of Missing Out)? Both are justifications for enjoying the "fun" things now and throwing caution into the wind for the future. In all transparency, I have had YOLO and FOMO, often, and do succumb to letting it lead me into "fun", oftentimes with negative consequences. The difference now is that, depending on the severity, I realize that I am gambling with my health. And that at any moment, the tide of life's choices could shift into unhealthy lifestyle consequences.

The decision to title this book *"INSPIRE Me, Ms. America! A Journey to Wellness con SABOR"* was strongly influenced by the interchange of that day almost 34 years ago. The struggle is real if we commit to a life of health and wellness. It's not just the struggle to push away food, it's much more than that. We sacrifice the "now" for the "later". But in this instance, I remember wondering? Could there be a happy medium? Could we eat food from Mrs. Alvarez's kitchen and still follow wellness guidelines? I think so and will use the remainder of this book to share how we can do that. You see, at my highest weight, I remember being 236 lbs and having an A1c or blood sugar level of 11.5, I had FOMO badly. We had just moved to a resort town and had financial stability like never before. As a couple we were surrounded by "friends", and we were invited to at least two social events every week. I remember investing in many formal dresses as I never wanted to be seen in the same dress twice. I spent years ``partying" to the point of allowing myself to become unhealthy. I would often share that I owned a mirror like that of Queen Mortilda from the Disney fairytale Snow White. When asked, "Who's the fairest of them all?" It never responded with anything other than "You are the fairest of them all". To put this into perspective, I should have weighed 155 lbs at maximum and a healthy blood sugar level should have been at A1c. 5.5. Simply put, I was in bad shape. My attitude was that I wanted to embrace life and do all that I could to enjoy it before I died and that was final! After all, my past life was grounded in poverty and lack and I owed it to myself to Carpe Diem, or seize the day. At my unhealthiest, I remember my mama commenting, "You are wearing your success on your body and it's not healthy." #TRUTH!

WHAT I LEFT OFF:

What this book is not about is body shaming or supporting a stereotype that states that one must be a size 8 to be accepted and considered beautiful. Believe me on this, every single one of you reading this book is beautiful, loved, and worthy. Do not accept comments or degrading remarks that say otherwise.

I ask you this one question and this ONE question only: Are you healthy? If you're a size 38 waist and are healthy, then I say "Hooray"!! You are beautiful. If you are a size 8 and are unhealthy and consumed with unhealthy eating patterns, then you may not be healthy and might need to address it, quickly. The body doesn't tell the whole story, it's as simple as that.

The premise for sharing these memoirs of my life and my struggle to reach maximum health and wellness began early on in childhood and has shaped who I am today. So, I invested over 72 months of my life in interviewing, researching, and documenting the disease of Type 2 Diabetes and its effects on quality of life. I found the common struggle is the same, to reach maximum health and wellness we must trade comfort foods for healthy foods, "Enchiladas for Broccoli", but I argue, does it have to be all of them? That is the question that *"INSPIRE Me, Ms. America! A Journey to Wellness con SABOR"*, will attempt to answer.

DISCLAIMER

I do not claim to be a medical professional, I know what has worked for me and I want to share it with you. I am on my own journey and my perspective around wellness is unique to me. These struggles of a diabetic are personal and deeply rooted in my past life-long journey.

WHY IS THERE SUCH AN URGENCY?

I believe in prevention and being proactive because it will save you. But how can you prevent something if you don't know much about it? Let's share our struggles and celebrations all the while managing or even reversing Type 2 Diabetes, con SABOR! Together we can plan, prepare and eat tasty, healthy meals that keep our blood sugar in the normal range and our bodies functioning well. They say that hindsight is 20/20 and if I had known what I know now, specifically during my days at Tierra Nuestra, I believe my "homegirls" in this picture would still be alive today because the little girl up front and I are the only two left to share this experience and that's a shame.

"The objective for the treatment of obesity is NOT weight loss but HEALTH gain." – **Carel Le Roux, Ph.D.**
Professor of Chemical Pathology, University College Dublin

Pictured Left to Right:

Top Row - La Negra (Mary), La Loca (Liz), Mama in Pink
Front Row - Me (La Osmond) to my left Linda (La Psycho,)
In front - Laura (No nickname), not part of the project and down at the front, Little Brown Sugar, (Marie)

What ever happened to Anna's Girl Scout Troop? She assembled the toughest, meanest, homegirls in the ghetto, who strutted green vests and collected fabric badges of honor. I chuckle about this time in my life as images of our oldest Girl Scout in the troop, lovingly named, La Loca or (Crazy lady), in her green vest come to mind. This was in 1971 when tattoos were not a favorable image. She had a message tattooed on her fore fingers for both hands that read, F.@.C.K., (right hand) and Y. O.U. <3, on the left hand. She never had to say a thing when she didn't agree with something, she simply clasped her fists together and pointed them in your face, and that was that. Although we never formally camped or "roughed it" out in the wilderness, we all agreed that being part of our neighborhood was roughing it quite enough, more on that later.

A Mexican Breakfast - Weekend Style:

Please see a modified version of this meal specifically altered for diabetics and featured at the end of the book.

t w o

LA CASA BLANCA & TIA LOVE

"Love is an emotion that we're capable of feeling in many different contexts-from intimate partner relationships and family bonds to friends and pets." **– Brene Brown,** *Atlas of the Heart*

Love is a complicated emotion and is foundational to optimum mental wellness. Musical lyrics deeply speak to the core of my emotions and I gravitate toward music with a positive love-centered message. Growing up in the Beatles era, their song "All You Need is LOVE", which first debuted in 1967, comes to mind.

"All You Need is Love"
Beatles

Chorus
All you need is love,
All you need is love,
All you need is love, love,
Love is all you need.

Whether you claim to be a Beatles fan or not, this song sings of a basic emotion that is foundational to our basic human needs. According to acclaimed American Psychology Professor and creator of the concept of basic human needs, Abraham Maslow, believed that all human beings aspire to become self-actualized. He continues to assert that this need is considered the highest motivating force, (see pyramid graph), of the five levels or Hierarchy of Human Needs, established by Maslow in 1962. It is surmised that we can not proceed to the higher level of human need until we first satisfy the current one. Starting at the base of the pyramid is, Psychological, then Safety, followed by Love/Belonging, then Esteem and finally Self-actualization, or the freedom to create one's own ideas. Each of these needs is shown on a smaller scale as we move upward. This indicates that the need is important but not as strong. His research included various conversations and interviews and he kept years of notes, 37 years to be exact. Including additional research, he established this pyramid Hierarchy of Human Needs.

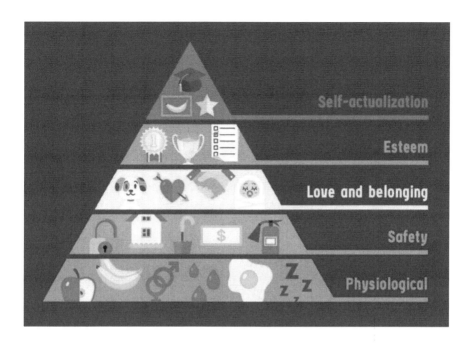

Undeniably, we can agree that as human beings we need to belong. We simply cannot survive without some sort of socialization where we love and belong to one another.

It is concerning that during the worldwide pandemic of 2020, statistics show us that we have now become the most anti-social societies in recent history. Believed to be for fear of contracting the disease of Covid-19 or other reasons, many of us have become "Me first" thinking, completely avoiding the need for community. In tragic situations, many go inward and begin again at the bottom of the pyramid at survival/ physiology. I am reminded of yet another song by the Black-Eye Peas, "Where Is the Love ", in which the lyrics confront us with the realities of loving mankind, even during crisis, political unrest, and social upheaval.

"Where Is the Love"
The Black-Eyed Peas

Chorus

People killing, people dying,
Children hurt and you hear them crying,
Can you practice what you preach?
And would you turn the other cheek?
Father, Father, Father help us,
Send some guidance from above,
Cause people got me, got me, questioning,
Where is the love?

We've all fallen victim to television news that updates us on the horrid realities of life. They are fixated on showing us the many failures of society. Highlighting tragedy after tragedy and examples of failed love. Watching this day-in-and-day-out, one could easily lose faith in humanity and the virtues of love, after all, isn't love supposed to be patient, and kind?

As you will read in the subsequent chapters, I am no novice to love lost. I have been emotionally hurt, physically hurt, felt betrayed and abandoned by those who claimed to love me, but I still have faith in the emotion.

I am convinced that all the world needs is love. The love between two humans is grown through the cultivation of words, actions, and descriptions of what they believe is loving. Once the communication is clear, it does not stop there as it is an ever-changing and ever-evolving emotion that requires maintenance for sustainability. My definition of love is much the same.

I still believe that love will prevail, I still believe in love's promises, and I still believe that love will make a way. I hope the following story will strengthen your belief in love, and I am confident that if we all err on the side of love, everything will be alright.

FOUR TYPES OF LOVE:

To set a reference point before we continue with this chapter, I'd like you to read the following definitions of the different types of love. Sit and ponder allowing someone in your life that fits that description, to come into your mind. The same person can double in different categories if you can't think of someone else. Search deep and even have a pen and paper to note their names and a line or two regarding how they have shown you love.

Should you have more than one person on your list per category of types of love, please count yourself as a very fortunate, favored and super-blessed person.

Philia Love - Deep friendship and affection but not romantic, mutual respect and understanding. The love that you feel for your "Bestie" or a Mentor.

Agape Love - Unconditional love that accepts the recipient regardless of their flaws. Loves without any regard for reciprocation. This is often described as the love that you would receive from God or a higher power.

Eros Love – Sensual or passionate love. This love is emotional, deep and fleeting.

Storge Love – (Greek) A natural love that family members have for one another. It is the type of love that parents feel toward their children and vice versa.

SISTER LOVE (STORGE & PHILIA)

We all need a support system, someone who cares enough to be there when called upon through the tough times in life. Someone who will love you with Philia love. I call it "*Sister-Friend*" love. A term coined by Maya Angelou, a famous American Poet who during her lifetime wrote a total of 29 books and was best known for her poem, "*And, Still I Rise*", published in 1978.

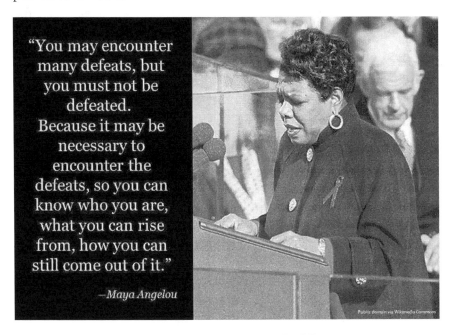

"You may encounter many defeats, but you must not be defeated. Because it may be necessary to encounter the defeats, so you can know who you are, what you can rise from, how you can still come out of it."

—Maya Angelou

Public domain via Wikimedia Commons

MY CHANGE-OF-LIFE-BABY

As I look back, I am so very grateful that my mother had three biological sisters who served as her Storge and Philia love: Tia Delia, Tia Rita, and Tia Eva. Tia means Aunt and for the remainder of this book, that is how I will refer to them. You may wonder where I am going with this and what it has to do with reversing diabetes. Well, hang on!

What I am about to share has quite literally been in my heart to put pen to paper for well over twenty years, long before ever learning that

I had acquired the horrible disease of Type 2 Diabetes (T2D). I knew, way back then, that I wanted to write a manuscript in honor of my Tias. The real "sister-love" of blood sisters who encircled my mother's life when she needed it most. The acts of love, kindness, and sacrifice shown to us, (me, my siblings and my mother) by these beautiful Tias, in short, saved our lives.

I was the first female, fourth in line of a total of five children born to my Mama. I had three older brothers, and some 9.5 years later we were blessed with a younger sister; my mother called her "my change-of-life baby". It is traditional, in the Latino culture, that the first-born female takes on the position of "mother-in-training". Women in our culture are oftentimes being groomed to take on the role of future wife/mother/caregiver. They have a saying in Spanish, "Una vez que aprendes a picar cebollas, te puedes casarte" which translated is, "Once you learn to mince the onion properly, you may marry." I am not quite sure how I feel about that statement, but there it is, nonetheless. Honestly, I don't remember much about this time in my life other than I was called upon to assist my mother every day of my young life while living at what I called La Casa Blanca, or the Big White House.

The following memories have been stored up in the deep recesses of my mind and when made to recall them, I feel intense emotions as they begin to surface. I find myself becoming emotionally exhausted after writing about this time. However, I push forward because I wholeheartedly believe that these experiences will help someone else to work through experiences of their own and eventually live a life of mental and physical wellness.

THE WHITE HOUSE WITH DARK MEMORIES

Growing up, we lived in a very old home on the West Side of San Jose, California. As mentioned it was a big white house with a covered porch resembling a farm-style design. My recall does not allow me to see or feel any warmth whatsoever about this memory, but rather just the sight of cold, hard cement. This house was very old and at present, I estimate it to be about 87 years old. It had a basement where the furnace was located causing the heat to rise from the vents in the floor on the main level. The kitchen had a large cast iron stove with an oven that was very difficult to cook on because the oven door was extremely heavy; just opening it took immense muscle strength. I remember this, distinctly, because I was taught my very first cooking lesson in that kitchen at nine years of age.

The Casa Blanca came with a "Casita" styled mini home in the backyard area. Complete with a small kitchen, bathroom, and a great-room style living and bedroom combo. Knowing what I now know about real estate in the present day, the house had very good "bones" and if it had been maintained correctly, could have been a nice investment for the family. In today's market, I estimate it to be worth about 2.3 million as it is located in what is now considered "The Silicon Valley" an area that has been modified, or one could say gentrified, for modern urban life. For me, the sad memories still seem to cloud over anything positive about the house.

Looking out the front windows of the white house and down the street to the right, there was a cocktail bar. This was my mama's "stomping grounds". A place she would frequent and also the place where she met my father. Oddly, the name of the bar was, "La Copa", which literally means "The Cup" but figuratively means "The Drink". I know now that my mother desperately needed to fill her emotional cup, often. It just so happens that her beverage of choice was filling her up with a substance that would eventually destroy her life. Her tonic of choice was beer and, on a special night, tequila. Both beverages would help her to mask layers of sadness and severe episodes of depression. Mental health professionals remark that to help patients with brain health issues, it requires years of extra therapy to peel back the layers of substance abuse that have been used to numb core issues of dysfunction. These substance abuse addictions oftentimes include drugs, alcohol, and overeating food, all of which cause damage to brain cells.

Across the street from that corner bar was the Del Monte Cannery. During the time of high operations, the cannery was bustling with traffic.

Seasonal workers would come and go and would often request to rent the basement of La Casa Blanca, for a short time. My mother was always in need of extra cash, so she would welcome a brief rental agreement. This all came to a screeching halt after the following incident.

SAVED BY MY PORCUPINE QUILLS, AKA MY VOICE

I used to love watching animals when I was a little girl. I remember asking my mother, how do they survive, once the mama stops looking after them? She responded, "God gives them each a way to defend themselves, like the porcupine. It has long quills that poke anything that is trying to hurt or eat them." This stuck with me as I was often left alone, for a few hours and up to a couple of days, and I remember thinking, "If something bad happens, how will I ever defend myself? My brothers were somewhat bullies to me. They hated me because I was Mama's favorite. Probably because I did everything at the house and they ran the streets. When they wanted to punch my arm or pull my hair, all I had to do was scream and they would plead for me to stop. It was great, just like a present-day superpower!

One day, I was playing outside by the driveway of the home, waiting for my family to arrive. Mama had several renters living in the basement. I was playing Dodgeball against the wall by myself. Then without notice, I was flagged over and coerced into entering the basement by a few male renter's. As I approached, I was invited to see the "new kittens" that had, apparently, just been born, so I eagerly followed. Once down the stairs and deep into the basement, I asked to see the kittens. That's when four men propositioned me to stay down there while one person went to "look" for them. Next, came an offer to have some candy. I began to feel uncomfortable as I did not see any kittens or candy. I felt scared and began to walk towards the exit door, it was then I noticed it was blocked by a big man who would not allow me to leave. Someone grabbed my arm and next, all I remember was immediately summoning my superpowers. Like a porcupine, I unleashed my defense mechanism; my loud voice as loud as I could. I remember that my screams could reach a soprano level that could shatter glass! Suddenly, I noticed my school friend, who had promised to come over and play, had arrived and noticed me in the basement screaming so he began to hit the glass window of the basement. The big man moved away from the doorway and I ran out. Jesusito was my savior that day. He stayed with me until an adult came home and during that time, the renters packed their bags and vacated the premises. After that day, my mother never had another renter in the home and boy was I happy about that.

Whenever I smell the stench of rotten tomatoes, it triggers me to those awful days while living in the big white house with dark shadows near the tomato cannery. Food labels with Del Monte logos or images I see in the grocery store can truly invoke a subliminal reaction. I find myself buying any other brand of canned tomato products available, even if they are more expensive. For me, the Del Monte brand has awful memories associated with it. Last I checked, the cannery is no longer operating and was replaced by a Silicon Valley business, good riddance!

At this time in my young life, being only ten years young, I remember praying to have both wisdom and riches. Wisdom, because I wanted to know how to best help my mama and riches because I knew that having money would lessen her stressful existence.

Then my sister arrived, and I was scared and unsure about what to do next as both my mama and my sister were not doing well. I felt like I was constantly on alert to care for my mother at a moment's notice and it was very stressful. I now know that there is a name for this extreme stress that I was experiencing, it's called childhood trauma.

Dr. Nadine Burke Harris, Founder of the Center for Youth Wellness, and current Surgeon General of California shares:

> The Centers for Disease Control and Kaiser conducted the Adverse Childhood Effects Study, ACEs, between 1995-1997. They were the first to examine the relationship between early childhood adversity and negative lifelong health effects. The research found that the long-term impact of ACEs determined future health risks, chronic disease, and premature death. Individuals who had experienced multiple ACEs also faced higher risks of depression, addiction, obesity, attempted suicide, mental health disorders, and other health concerns. It also revealed that ACEs were surprisingly common—almost two-thirds of respondents, part of the largely white, well-off sample, reported at least one ACE.

> "Childhood trauma increases the risk for **seven out of ten** of the leading causes of death in the United States. In high doses, it affects brain development, the immune system, hormonal systems, and even the way our DNA is read and transcribed. Folks who are exposed to very high doses have triple the lifetime risk of heart disease and lung cancer and a **20-year difference** in life expectancy."

ACES can have lasting effects on....

Health (obesity, diabetes, depression, suicide attempts, STDs, heart disease, cancer, stroke, COPD, broken bones)

Behaviors (smoking, alcoholism, drug use)

Life Potential (graduation rates, academic achievement, lost time from work)

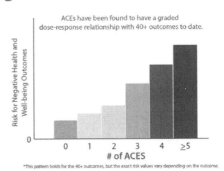

For the next few months, I became the primary caregiver for my newborn baby sister. I remember my mother teaching me to change her diaper. And, for the first time ever I saw it! A dry crusty piece of skin with a black-colored center, that I later understood to be dried blood! It was a vivid memory; my sister's partial umbilical cord was still attached! When I saw it, I let out a loud yell and screamed at the sight, "Ewwwe, What's THAT?", I asked. The response was, "It's part of her belly button and will fall off soon. If it does, and you find it in the diaper, just throw it away", said Mama. In addition to diaper changing, I learned to wash cloth diapers; including hanging them to dry using old-school wooden clothespins, and a wire clothesline that resembled connected guitar strings. Later, I found out that my observations were right. The clothesline consisted of used guitar strings that had broken during use and were donated to the family by my youngest uncle, Pablo. He was an aspiring guitar player for a musical band and whenever he had to restring his guitar, he would donate the used ones to us for clothesline repair. I also learned to make baby formula using condensed milk, boiled water, and Karo brand syrup. To this day the smell of baby formula turns my stomach. The first disposable diapers were introduced in the late 1940s, but they only became popular for use in America in the early 1970s. This was a luxury item that we simply could not afford. I was the little mama, at 10 years young, and to this day I still slip and may refer to my sister as "mija", which in Spanish is the condensed version of Mi Hija or my daughter.

BRAIN HEALTH AND DEPRESSION

My beautiful Mama was struggling with depression. Postpartum depression from the recent birth of my sister and brain health complications that were never fully diagnosed or treated from a past car accident she was in during her teen years, more on that to come.

Currently, I am a small business owner who specializes in Team Building, Leadership skills and most recently, Brain Health and Mental Wellness in the workplace. Most participants who attend my training courses on Brain Health and Wellness are quickly convinced that they need what I'm teaching and immediately ask what to do next. They comment, "Okay Dolores, we get it, now what do we do?" My response is, "Honestly, it's so simple, you're going to say, 'That's all?'" Brain Health specialists advise that taking care of our mental health requires daily lifestyle changes. And, preventative maintenance. They recommend we practice the following six behaviors at a minimum and have coined it **"SIX to FIX"**:

1. **Hydration:** (No, not Gatroade) Drink half your weight in ounces. Clean, clear water daily, (150lbs = 75oz).

2. **Rest:** Sleep a minimum of 7 hours a night. If this is hard to do, begin an evening ritual and stick to it until your "circadian rhythm" begins to respond.

3. **Movement:** Move, a minimum of 30 minutes a day, at an increased heart rate.

4. **Eat:** Whole foods including vegetables and fruits. If you're craving a banana cream pie, chances are that you just really need a banana.

5. **Limit Extras:** alcohol, recreational drugs, and processed sugar, once in a while or better off, never. (Full transparency, I am still in the once-in-a-while camp).

6. **Prayer and Meditation,** we have got to spend some time alone with ourselves and with a creator or higher power, if you will, because there is a spiritual aspect to our brain health that we cannot ignore.

The suggestions really haven't changed much over the years and have really only been rebranded or packaged differently. What has happened is that our society has adopted the YOLO mentality, (You Only Live Once) and I believe it is directly related to the aftershocks from the pandemic. We are simply not taking medical prevention seriously and the consequences are horrendous. By not actively becoming involved in lifestyle changes, whole families are being destroyed. So do we have to eat like the "Gabachos"? I say no and if you continue reading to chapter seven, you'll understand why.

If we practice these SIX to FIX behaviors, we can quite literally push back the effects of chronic diseases. Sadly, mama was doing it all wrong! She very rarely drank water and instead substituted it for alcohol to numb her emotional pain. She slept sporadically due to a newborn sleep schedule and to being out well into the morning hours. She moved a bit but not consistently. I, honestly, don't remember having vegetables on my plate as a child. What we did have in the refrigerator instead of vegetables, was processed foods, hot dogs, Hamburger Helper, chips, milk & cereal, and ICE CREAM. YUMMY! Ice cream was my favorite comfort food.

THE TURNING POINT

On this particular evening, I recall it started out as a good day for my mother. She was up and moving around and even asked me to bring my baby sister to her as she sat on the window seat and looked out the window. Even though her depression would now ebb and flow, she tried to remain optimistic. That day, I noticed her looking at herself in the mirror, often, moving her jet-black hair up and down to test out different hairstyles. She asked me to look for her ruby red lipstick because she had misplaced it. I was allowed to try some on myself and thought that I looked like a movie star.

Later that evening she sprung up from the bed and professed that she needed some "adult time". I knew what that meant; a walk to the corner bar.

Even after giving birth to five children, my mother remained very attractive. A round, pear-shaped, light-skinned lady, with a huge smile and boisterous demeanor. She would describe herself as "Lizbeth Taylor", just like that, "Lizbeth" not "Elizabeth". She was also very voluptuous. With a full-figure hourglass shape, DD-size breasts, and a narrow waist. She always wore classy clothes and long sleeve blouses to hide her "bad arm". That was the arm she was unable to move any longer because of her childhood accident. It would just hang there with little to no circulation and was smaller in size than her right arm and hand.

It was 1970, she was 39 years young, a single parent, disabled, and now had five kids, and no husband! Honestly, I probably would have been depressed myself. On this particular day, I remember she had been dealing with bouts of depression crying off and on. What started as a good day ended with Mama becoming very "anxious". My newborn baby sister had a cold and a stuffy nose. She was hungry but could not drink properly from her bottle without needing to come up for air after sucking only a few ounces of milk, which made her agitated.

It was a cold Saturday evening in October, my sister had finally fallen asleep. I had been catering to my mom all day, as she would describe, "waiting on me hand and foot". I watched as she combed her hair, and put on some red lipstick and fancy clothes. A baby blue colored pants suit with some kind of sequence that sparkled on her blouse. My mother was always one for the "bling" look. What's funny is the older I get, the more I look for that type of clothing style. I remember promising my younger self that I would never want to look like my mother.

As she walked toward the door, she looked back and assured me she would be home before my baby sister woke up. Immediately, I went into mini-mama mode and checked on supplies just in case I had to make more formula. I did not want to have to go look for my mother when she was out because cell phones had not been invented therefore once she was gone, she was gone. Needing her would require me to walk to the corner bar and call out her name from the entrance door. The sign clearly said, "No Children Allowed!" and they meant it! Before this particular day, this walk to the corner was something I remember doing frequently.

I genuinely don't know how she managed to get it, but my mother owned a beautiful Sky Blue '54 Chevy Impala Super Sport with a white Convertible top. I think that it was willed to her by my grandfather but I'm not quite sure. All I know is that it was an attention grabber, for sure. As the day progressed, it was getting late, so I finally looked out the window to see if I could catch a glimpse of my mama walking toward the house from La Copa. That's when I noticed the car was gone. Immediately I panicked! My oldest brother was detained at the Boy's Ranch for minimal crimes that today would receive no more than a slap on the wrist, and my other two brothers were "running the streets" trying to find trouble; they were always successful. I was left alone with my sister. As fate would have it, she woke up and screamed for milk because she was hungry. I remember giving her a few sips of formula, here and there, until we both fell asleep. I was praying for God to bring my mother home as soon as possible. That's when I heard it, a loud BANG that was so loud it shook the whole house. I was startled because it sounded like and felt like an Earthquake. Frozen and scared, I decided not to investigate and to just move to a safer place in the house with my sister to hide and pray. I must have fallen back to sleep because I don't remember hearing anything else for about two hours. It was then that my mother walked into the house stumbling and doing her best to stay standing. I immediately noticed her bloody nose and what I now know to be urine stains on her beautiful blue pantsuit. She had wet herself in the crash. Two hours prior she had been so drunk that as she turned into the driveway of the house, traveling at too fast a pace, she lost her grip on the steering wheel and hit the side of the house, where the chimney was located, and wrecked her car. She said she must have hit her head on the steering wheel and passed out. When she walked into the house, she saw us both wide-eyed and scared out of our minds. I remember the first words out of her mouth were, "I promise never to drink again". At the time I had no idea what that statement would do for our family, I was just glad that she was home.

The next day, after she had sobered up, she cried even more than she had days before and kept saying "That could have been a person that I hit instead of the chimney, and I would have never forgiven myself." I believe that incident had such a deep impact on her because 22 years prior she had been the victim of a serious car accident. A car hit her as she walked across a busy intersection in the Mission District of San Francisco. That accident forever changed her life, more on that later. As her first move to make good on her promise, my mama went to church and signed a written agreement with a Catholic Priest to never touch liquor again.

HERE COMES THE LOVE!

47

Almost like a scene from the Mary Poppins movie, as she comes to help Mr. and Mrs. Banks with life, somehow the calvary was called in, uninvited, the sisters came in from far and near and seemed to have arrived all at the same time. I may be over-exaggerating the scene but that's how I felt. With food and cleaning supplies in hand, they got started on repairing the damage that years of neglect had caused. They also had suitcases for the forced visit we were about to take to their homes.

Let's get this clear, I am not speaking of Sisters from a Convent but from her family. My Aunts (Tias) entered the scene. These sisters found out what was happening with my mother and quickly came to the rescue. They all converged at our house, having traveled over 50 miles to get there and did not allow my mother to refuse their help or to act as if everything was alright.

One arrived and began to clean the house. Another came with a few bags of groceries and prepared food. The third sister simply took time to care for the five of us. She washed our clothes and forced us to take showers. Winter break was nearing, so the third Tia began making vacation plans to take us away from our mother for a few weeks until she could get her life in order. From that day forward, until we became teenagers and had a choice of our own, I remember our vacation days being spent in the Bay Area, surrounded by our cousins and a "normal" way of life.

The love of food is deeply rooted in our family. For us, food is love, and if you share it with someone, you sacrifice much. Much of this love for food con SABOR, comes from the advice, counsel, and mentorship of my Tias. Tia Delia was the firstborn of the extended family. She had style and class and took on the role of "little Mama" as mentioned earlier in the book. She was married to a San Francisco Police Officer for 45 years before he passed away. She was a lover of Italian food. But what I remember most was her work ethic. Religiously, she would get up and take the city bus to the factory to complete her tasks as a machine operator. She was a true "Rosie the Riveter". A Machine Operator during WWII, she loved to walk to the local market or Fisherman's

Wharf for some fresh Boudins Sourdough Bread, which is original to San Francisco. I remember, during Christmas or Summer vacations, we would walk everywhere, up and down the streets of Daly City. She lived in a house that was connected to the neighbor's house and looked like a Victorian home. It had a cool basement, not like the scary one in the home of my childhood.

Next in the birth order of women was my mom but we'll skip her and go on to my Tia Rita. Like Tia Delia, Tia Rita was a beautiful lady. She always took good care of her hair, nails, and skin. She lived in South San Francisco and because her second husband held a position of esteem, and had a high-paying job, she was able to work part-time. She lived in a home up in the foothills and from her backyard, through the second-floor window of my cousin's bedroom, a scenic view of the sunrise over the Bay could be seen on clear mornings. Tia Rita loved to cook and made fresh tasty meals every night. She mostly cooked like the Anglo-Americans because her second husband was white. I remember she taught me how to cook Prime Rib, new potatoes, and broccoli. She tried to convince me that the red part of the meat was good, not raw, but I still saw it as a bloody mess and did not want to partake. She and I had very similar personality styles and loved similar things. The Autumn season was especially exciting to us both and I remember her now, fondly, as the Autumn leaves begin to turn colors. She was a good listener and would ask me many open-ended questions. Questions that required my opinion and made me feel important and like I mattered. Best of all, she remembered special things I said, like my favorite color or TV show, and would repeat them back to me at a later date, even months later. When I was with her, I was not in panic mode and I felt like I could truly rest.

As far as my cooking skills, Mexican food in particular, I truly owe my skills and talent to the youngest of the three sisters, Tia Eva. She and my grandmother taught me how to make a variety of homemade dishes. I continually give credit to these women and to what they taught me because it was my cooking that won over my husband of 41 years. Flour tortillas, Chile Verde, Tamales, Mexican Rice, Frijoles de la Olla (pot beans) and so much more. Not so good for the current-day Diabetic, but that is the premise of why I wrote this book. If we truly want to sustain a healthy way of life, we need to consider traditions, lifestyles, culture, and SABOR and incorporate them all into our plan for health and wellness. I believe we can still have tasty, flavorful food from our past by modifying the way we prepare and serve it to our loved ones.

LOVE IS A VERB!

My Tia Eva lived in Sunnyvale and was the mother of five. Her two oldest children would become some of my closest cousins. Ironically, Tia Eva's home was located in a town named Sunnyvale, which to me sounded very happy, but beneath the surface was an environment that was quite the contrary. Unfortunately, there was an undertone of traumatic relationships going on in that environment but as a kid, I decided to ignore it and continued having fun with my cousins. My Tia Eva was beautiful, so generous, and an all-around amazing person. She cared for everyone who was in need. I often referred to her as a "culinary magician". When her pantry was very sparse, she could turn a pot of freshly boiled pinto beans, five potatoes, one beef steak, three cans of tomato sauce, a sack of flour, lard, and some vermicelli pasta or what we called Fideo, into a meal fit for a king. Her family alone required seven mouths to feed, every evening. Then she would graciously open her doors to those in need, like me, my brothers, and sometimes even neighbors. That would bring the total to an average of 14 hungry adolescents. From the ingredients just mentioned above she could prepare a meal like the following:

- » **Guisado de Chile Colorado con Papas** - Meat and potatoes with Red Chile sauce.
- » **Fideo Pasta** - Vermicelli pasta sautéed in lard, almost to a crispy brown texture with 1/4 of a cup of tomato sauce and a sprinkle of sharp cheddar cheese.
- » **Pinto Beans** – boiled with a left-over ham hock.

» **Homemade Flour Tortillas** - with butter. I remember the stack of tortillas was sky-high!
» **And Salsa** – plenty of fresh salsa al molcajete.

I think back and share these memories with total and complete appreciation. If it hadn't been for these angels on Earth, who took it upon themselves to save us five children, their nieces, and nephews, I don't know what would have become of us. They exhibited both Storge and Philia love and it encircled us for our lifetime.

I am confident that my mother would have never reached out to my Tias on her own. It's tough admitting you have an addiction, especially to family members. Vulnerability and shame are difficult emotions to handle and come to terms with, but my mama loved us more than her pride and accepted their help.

My Tias came in with nothing but love and taught me many things about myself, my hygiene, and an appreciation for work and life. Every Summer for many years after, I was carted around to each Tia's house for several weeks. They would take me shopping and to museums and such.

We'd often frequent Fisherman's Wharf and at present, whenever I visit San Francisco and ride on the trolley cars, I think of my Tias and shed a few tears in grateful praise. One final note I'd like to make is that now, as an adult, I know that two of the three Tia's had full-time jobs. They were so committed to helping us through this time in our lives that they would reserve their vacation days and save extra funds to share with us when we'd come to visit because they knew my mother lacked the money to purchase the basic items we needed for the upcoming school year. More importantly, they would share quality time with us while filling us up with love, affirmations, and hope. Then, after our Summers away, we were sent back to our mother. In today's world, I want to believe that the family unit is just as tight, but that may not be true. We may be losing that quality as we move away from a family-centered focus. I hope that we can recognize and reverse that trend.

three

MS. AMERICA AND THE WHITE SWAN

"I AM_____, two of the most powerful words, for what you put after them shapes your reality" – **Unknown**

I heard it said, "What you believe you are is more important than what others think you are." That statement has relevance but it made little sense to me when I was a little girl. The image I had was shaped primarily by what the adults around me thought of me. If my loved ones told me that I was a toad, I would have believed them and tried my darndest to hop around the house as the best dang toad in the world.. Kidding aside, as a child with no daddy in the home, a part-time mama due to her addiction, and three older brothers who were never home, what I believed of myself was formed by my prior experiences. No social media, no TV, or very little, anyway. I was alone a lot.

Food became my friend. I remember that a single quarter would be enough to buy a feast of my favorite junk foods. So I'd canvass the streets looking for empty Coke bottles and redeeming them at the corner store, a delicatessen named Paradiso's Italian Deli. This was my "go-to" for fast food. At my young age, I was resourceful. No food in the house, no problem. Once I was able to save a quarter, it would be enough to buy a bag of barbecue chips, 10 cents, a single-wrapped Reese's peanut butter cup candy, 5 cents, and a Big Stick Ice Pop, another 10 cents. All my food cost me a whooping 25-cent piece!! That was in the "Stone Age", nonetheless, that food made me happy for a while.

I think back now and understand the importance of nutritional options for healthy brain development in children but in this neighborhood, the options were very limited. No vegetables, fruits, or protein bars, like the millions of options of protein bars that can be found in today's mini-marts. Granted, there were deli sandwiches at Paradiso's Italian Deli, but we couldn't afford them. Sociologists would have deemed my neighborhood a true food desert.

What is a "Food Desert?" A food desert is an area where getting fresh, healthy foods like fruits, vegetables, and whole grains is especially difficult. They can be found in urban and rural areas and often include communities of color with low income. They are typically located in areas where people often do not own a car. While public transportation can assist these people in some instances, often economic flux has driven grocery stores out of the city and into the suburbs. See the link for more information. *www.povertyusa.org/stories/homeless-food-deserts-losangeles*

With a bar, La Copa, across the street, and a cannery to the left of the store, the Deli catered to customers who needed a quick sandwich and offered snack foods, sodas, and liquor, of course. I was an overweight kid and not well-kept. I was very resourceful and found ways to survive. Chronologically, at this time, my sister had not been born yet. I was about eight years young, give or take, and my grandparents lived with us in the back house or "Casita" of La Casa Blanca. Even though I was alone in the big house, most of the time, the grandparents were only a stone's throw away. During my foundational years, my grandparents were the core of my security and we spent much of our free time together. We'd watch all of the popular evening shows together. The Lawrence Welk Show reruns, I Dream of Jeannie, and many other American shows that premiered in the mid-1960s were some of our favorites. Lawrence Welk was known for Big Band music and his legacy was the song Tiny Bubbles which my grandfather loved to dance to.

My grandmother only spoke Spanish and I remember that she took it upon herself to cook for us, every day, they didn't have much to speak of, but they always had food for us. Thinking back, I believe that it was an unwritten agreement that they would stay at the casita rent-free and, in return, they would watch over us kids. One of my brothers was in Little League Baseball. He was often asked for proof of age because at ten years old he already stood 5'10 in height. Our grandfather would make it a point to go to every one of his games, and like Mookie Betts from the Los Angeles Dodgers, he'd consistently make a home run in almost every game. It was a sure bet that you would smell homemade fried potatoes, freshly made for my brother before he left for the game. The aroma of fresh salsa, fried potatoes, and pinto beans would permeate their little studio and float up to the big white house and that was my signal to make my way over to the casita because food was about to be put on the table.

LIFELONG COMMITMENT

My grandmother was just 14 years young, and my grandfather was 19 years old when they were married. He stole her from her mother, (her words, not mine), and they ran away to an adjacent town in the state of Texas to get married by the Justice of the Peace. It wasn't until their 25th wedding anniversary that they had a proper wedding ceremony that ended up being one of four total. When they reached 50 years, they had another blessing ceremony and then again another huge ceremony at their 75th wedding anniversary. By that time, counting family members alone, not including guests, the attendance would reach 100 plus, easily. My grandfather, without fail, loved to make his grand speech each time we gathered. He asked all the blood relatives to stand. He'd then proceed to say "You see all these people standing at this moment?" He'd look around the room slowly and seemed to shed a tear. Then he would say, with his chest puffed up, with a proud crackly voice, "Everyone here came from us and he'd proceed to point to grandma." "Our love, between you and your Mama, (meaning grandma) started it all." Everyone would break out in a roar of applause and he'd sit down and not say too much more for the rest of the evening. It was a pleasant moment for the over 50-75 blood relatives who were standing on their feet.

Over the years my grandmother learned a bit more English and I, more Spanish, so we were able to communicate much better. Just after the Priest blessed their 75-year matrimony, I went over to ask her how she felt about celebrating the wedding ceremony. What transpired next would affect the image I had of my timid, wholesome grandmother, for the rest of my life.

I asked, "Grandma, how do you feel, now that you've been married again?" Grandmother thought that each time she was "blessed" by a priest, she understood it to be another wedding. By then my grandma was 89 years of age and she and my grandfather had seven adult children, 29 grandchildren, and 19 great-grandchildren. She went on to say, "I married for the first time when I was 14, then 39, then 64, now 89 years old, right? I looked around me and noticed a crowd beginning to gather around her as she sat in her wheelchair. They seemed to wait for her response with bated breath and didn't want to miss the wisdom she was about to impart to multiple generations. I supposed that we were all waiting to hear a statement in support of marriage and some nuggets of advice, after all, not too many people can say that they had been married for 75 years! I responded, "Yes, you've been celebrated four times." Grandma then looked around as if she was looking for someone. I suspect that she was looking for my grandfather. When she felt that the coast was clear, she asked, "But why?" I responded, "Huh? But why, what do you mean, Grandma?"

Then she hit us with the real grandma, and it was like a bowling ball that just knocked down all of the bowling pins, hard. She continued, "Yeah, but why to the same man, I was hoping for a different one each time, someone younger." My mouth opened wide, and I felt my tongue hit the ground, figuratively speaking of course. There was a release of laughter and all I can say is, I've never been the same since. FYI, they managed to reach their 77th wedding anniversary before my grandma passed. They lived in their home and cared for each other with minimal outside assistance until she left this world. My mother and the other siblings were able to help care for them, on a rotation basis, when needed. And no, she never got married again to that younger man.

Let's put a pause on the past for a minute and clarify something. My life wasn't peaches and cream, but children are resilient, and their brains

can adapt and rebound quickly. The situations are all very different and related to the type of trauma and severity of the living situations, but for me, having my grandparents close by was my saving grace.

A MIND-IN-ACTION

Do you know that the mind and the brain are two different elements of mental health yet their functions are interconnected? For so many years, I thought those two systems were the same. But, I now know they are absolutely not. Put simply, the mind is the creative function, and the brain is the biological function. If you stay in a particular thought pattern for too long, scientists say that your brain will follow suit, and eventually your body will react by attempting to perform whatever action has been in your thoughts for too long. Of course, there is self-control, but the point here is that once a thought crosses your mind it affects the brain and can become an action.

My initial interest in mental wellness began because of the diagnosis of brain health issues for one of my children, bipolar disorder to be exact. I was adamant about learning all there was to learn about these health challenges. It didn't happen right away but once it set in, I realized I needed to get involved.

You are beeautiful.

"You never have to settle or just learn to compensate… There are so many things you can and should do to alter, change, slow down, and even reverse the current state of your brain and body. These things are mind-driven: they're the result of your choices, which are the results of your feelings, which are the result of your thinking. This is the mind-in-action."

Dr. Caroline Leaf - Communication Pathologist and Neuroscientist

Dr. Leaf's passion includes helping people see the power of the mind to change the brain, control chaotic thinking, and find mental peace. She is the author of *Think and Eat Yourself Smart* and many other books and articles. She states, "My life's mission is to help people realize how much power they have in themselves to heal their minds, brains, and bodies. You may not have access to a therapist, but you have something more powerful, your mind."

Granted, the odds were stacked against me growing up, but knowing the information about the brain and the mind that I now know, I plan on fulfilling my destiny to share the knowledge about brain health with others.

DADDY VS. FATHER

"Mama, why does everyone have a daddy except me?" I am sure that my mother was tired of hearing me ask that question over and over again. I didn't know it at the time, but I envied anyone who got to have a special relationship with their daddy. If you are a product of a single-family head of the household, then I don't have to tell you the difference between the two terms, "Father" and "Daddy". But briefly, a father equals the biological aspect of creating a child and a daddy is someone who sticks around, through thick and thin, and nurtures a child to become a strong individual ready for what life has to offer. That is my definition based on what I knew. I am sure there is a more professional definition, but it is how I learned to understand it. Either way, I had a father and not a Daddy. He would frequent La Copa and meet up with my mother when he was in town. You see he was a workaholic and drove across different states to deliver oil barrels and honestly, that's all I really knew about him. He did provide for us as he paid for his share of child support for all three of his children with my mother, consistently. He was also a functioning alcoholic, therefore, if he was not working, he was drinking.

THE GRACEFUL SWAN

One evening, I recall my mama summoning me across the house to come into the living room area. She had a happy tone in her voice, and I remember wanting to cherish that moment, so I ran to her in excitement. It was then that I met him for the first time, my father. He was a handsome man, resembling that of a very tired and weather-worn Clark Gable. Sitting on our couch finishing up a Pall Mall cigarette. I remember this moment well because the cigarette had no filter and he had very calloused fingertips and was able to put it out using his thumb.

When I walked into the room he stood up and my mother introduced me to a man I knew nothing about. As a young girl, I did not have the emotional vocabulary to respond immediately so I just stood there and then I felt tears coming down my cheeks, but I wasn't sobbing. He then reached out to me for a hug and said, "Mija, eres muy bonita" translated, "Daughter, you are very pretty". I recall him having the same color eyes as mine, a light-brown hazel type. No one else in the family had that color of eyes. I knew now that my father and I matched.

My mama's words meant the world to me, it was all I had. I remember on that same occasion of meeting my father for the first time, my mother asked me to go get my fake Tiara made of foil paper and come in when she began to sing "our song". She stressed that I should come in like "a graceful swan, slow and with your head high." Then, she began…

There she is, Miss America
There she is, you're ideal
The dreams of a million girls
Who are more than pretty
May come true in Atlantic City
Oh she may turn out to be
The queen of femininity
There she is, Miss America
There she is, your ideal
With so many beauties
She'll take the town by storm
With her all-American face and form
And there she is
Walking on air she is
Fairest of the fair she is
Miss America

"There She is Miss America"
Sung annually at the Miss America Pageant since 1955 by Bert Parks,
until 2013

Written by Bernie Wayne

I believed EVERY WORD!

"When parents feel negatively toward themselves, it is equally easy for them to extend these feelings to their children. The negative thoughts parents harbor toward themselves can lead to parental rejection, neglect, or hostility. Not only are parents more likely to be critical of their offspring in ways that are similar to the ways they are disapproving of themselves, but their negative self-esteem also serves as an example for their children. As kids grow up, they often take on their parents' negative self-perceptions and the critical point of view directed toward them. For example, if a parent regards their child as a burden, that attitude will be woven into the child's self-esteem."

Your child's self-esteem starts with you!
– Lisa Firestone, Ph.D., Psychology Today - 2013

I never felt like my mother channeled her low self-esteem onto me. She also never allowed my brothers to bad-mouth me or call me ugly or fat. They certainly did when we were alone but not while my mother was present.

If my mother told me that I was as beautiful as Miss America, then that's what I was. "I am_____a beauty queen!"

Growing up my daughter would often question me as to why she did not get my eye color and my response was always, "I would give up my eye color in a second to have had a daddy like yours, any day."

I would go on to see my father only a handful of times throughout my adolescent and teen years, then he passed away in my late twenties from kidney issues due to his addiction and organ deterioration by Type 2 Diabetes.

The pressures of my young life were getting heavy for me. I was tired of wondering where we'd get the next meal. I was getting tired of being worried for my brothers who were out running the streets, and mostly I was getting tired of not knowing when my mama would get better. I wasn't the only one who was tired. My grandparents decided to move to another location because they were tired of enabling my mother's unhealthy lifestyle. Then came the notice that in just a few months, we'd have another member of the family. Not knowing the true repercussions of this news, I was so very excited, but my mother was more nervous. Disabled at 15 years young, now in her late 30s, 39 to be exact, she was unmarried and about to have her fourth child with no daddy to speak of. Nevertheless, we battled on and waited for the new baby to be born.

THE LIBERATED WOMEN - TIMES WERE CHANGING

The new food craze of the mid-60s was "fast" everything. The ultimate in convenience foods was all the craze. I remember having my first TV dinner, and drinking SODA! Tab soda, to be exact. It was sugar-free and since that was my first experience with a soft drink my palette got used to that taste and since then, I really can't drink regular soda. And, then there was TANG! How about TANG? The orange juice substitute that had no orange juice in it at all, but was so popular that advertisers boasted astronauts took it with them up into space! Well as you would probably guess, with my grandparents gone and out of the picture, those freshly cooked dinners were as well.

At the time, there was a new food delivery service that would come to your home once you subscribed. It could be likened to an Amazon of the '60s, the only difference was that you had to order what you needed for the following week when they delivered your current food order.

It was a limited menu, but my mother taught me how to order. Eggs, milk, cheese, ice cream, and several different processed meats would come to the home once a week. The driver was a pleasant man and would arrive in his small, refrigerated truck with a big white logo on the side of the freezer, it was a huge white swan. You guessed it, the company was called SCHWAN's Home Delivery! Somehow, they took pity on my mother and allowed her to be the first customer who could purchase food on credit. That act of kindness to extend food on credit to us helped us to survive through this time.

THE STATE INTERVENES

As I was writing this part of the book, I often felt nauseated and just really tired. I wear a CGM, Continuous Glucose Monitor, that tracks my blood sugar. Over the past few days, the numbers had been consistently high for no reason. I had been eating well and exercising, however, it seems that writing down memories from an emotionally suppressed time of my life caused my blood sugar to spike from stress. It is so easy to push down painful memories. To support what Dr. Leaf stated about the brain/mind connection, I haven't let my mind think about this time in a while so my body reacted.

One of my last memories of this time in my life was the intervention by the State of California and County Child Protective Services. Here is where my memories begin to blur. My mother was still pregnant, and we were waiting for the baby to be born. By then she had slowed her "gallivanting" as she would say, due to being close to giving birth. A representative from the state came to visit and evaluate the home. I remember we were almost removed from the home and placed with family members due to the poor living conditions. My mother was able to convince them to leave us with her and return in a week. The following days into the week, we would clean and organize like our life depended on it, because it did. Being that she was now sober, my mother had a clear view of what needed to be done and she had all of us getting busy doing it.

As promised, the Child Protective Services worker assigned to our case walked into our home for the second time that month and complimented us on the tidy appearance. He went on to say that he would be visiting us weekly until after the baby was born. I will never forget this man. He was a tall man in his mid-twenties. Blonde hair, blue eyes, and a very kind demeanor. He seemed to show empathy for our situation. One of the many goals he had for us was to teach us to cook healthy meals and to incorporate more fruits and vegetables into our meals. I remember eating chicken & broccoli for dinner and cantaloupe melon. It was presented with a scoop of vanilla ice cream in the center of a half melon as dessert, and I was okay with that! The future wasn't all roses yet, but during this time we or I was able to have a rest from the turmoil and stress. By the way, our Case Worker's name was... wait for it: Ken **Swan** - Social Worker/Nutritionist.

four

THE "BONITA" BRAIN

"I believe in YOU and ME." – **Sandy Linzer**
Sung by Whitney Houston & Berry Manilow

Her intellect level and word recall were off the charts since just toddler age. She felt emotions deeply and was extremely sensitive and loving. She was an avid reader and a quiet competitor to her older brother by 2.5 years. As an adult, she has blossomed into a strong person who followed her love of books to become a Librarian with a master's degree, she's an author, doggy parent, and an all-around warrior for injustices. Beautiful to the tilt, and an all-around amazing person, it is for her that I have titled this chapter The Bonita Brain, "Bonita" in Spanish, means beautiful. In short, she is the reason why I began researching brain health and have begun my mission to spread the news to the masses, firstly starting with this book.

THE TASMANIAN DEVIL AND OVERLOAD

I remember, during a time when I was feeling particularly overwhelmed, I shared with my kids: "Mama has a lot on her plate." And boy did I. I was juggling a very demanding, full-time job. I was managing our home, supporting all the various school activities, and I was taking care of my ailing mother. As a strong "Doer" personality, I had always been able to do it all, with confidence. At the time, I wasn't quite sure any longer. The Doer personality is oftentimes described as someone who gets things done, just as the name implies. But, one of the downsides of this personality is that in getting busy completing one's tasks, the Doer tends to be "pushy" and domineering. The area of improvement for this personality type is to work on improving their listening skills as they are often compared to the Looney Tunes character, introduced in 1930's, Tasmanian Devil, who travels by rapidly spinning. He would spin into a situation, stop, look around for something interesting, then grunt, decide it was time to go, and spin out and away, never paying much attention to anything that was not urgent. I felt like my life at the time was much like that. I only had enough time to handle the emergencies. I am sure that many can relate.

As a manager, I was in a newly created position where the focus was on profitability. I had a group of eight leaders on my team and our actions were constantly being evaluated. Literally every morning at our business unit report out, we'd stand in front of a large dry-erase board and present our productivity numbers from the prior day, while the other manager would ask for clarification. I believe I was the first female who was Latina that was a Continuous Improvement Manager in the history of this reputable food manufacturing plant. I was new to the engineering side of the job but not to creating solid working relationships with employees and that was my element of focus for the over one-thousand-member team. My task was to create a bridge between the Research and Development Engineers who spent much of their time up in their glass window offices, away from the front-line packers and sorters on the plant floor.

In addition, my mother had recently come to live with us because her health was rapidly declining and she was in poor condition. In her quest to be independent, she ignored self-care and did not stay strong. Our family decided to move her into our home permanently and to have a new home built that allowed for a "mother-in-law quarters". That way, she was still independent but had us nearby in case of emergencies.

Also at this time, my two older teens were in high school, and our youngest was in elementary school. My husband was very patient and helpful but he was dealing with a very demanding job as well, so we were all just trying to stay above water. I needed help and while I did get some relief from friends and family, most of it came from a special friend, Melissa, whom I met while she was in high school. She was the one that came to my rescue. We immediately became close friends; I promised to be her mentor to help her achieve her goal of entering college and she, in turn, would be our live-in nanny while attending school at the nearby college. I was excited because she was like me in that she would be the first in her family to step foot on a college campus.

MY DAILY DEMANDS (IN ORDER OF PRIORITIES)

In full transparency, and trying to hold back apologies or feelings of shame, this is how I organized the top seven priorities in life. At the time, I felt that there was no other way. If I could add a sad emoji here I would.

1. Work
2. Children
3. Mama
4. Home Management
5. Husband
6. Me (Self-Care)
7. God

BLINDSIDED BY MENTAL ILLNESS A TRUE T.K.O.

I recall this day like no other in my life and compare it to being unexpectedly hit, blindsided by a football, traveling at warp speed, or to being punched extremely hard on the side of my head and being, what boxers call, a total knockout TKO!

"Hello Mrs. Neira, this is your daughter's school counselor. Can you please come to the school as soon as possible, your daughter is in the Nurse's office." I immediately thought to myself, I don't remember her complaining of a cold or showing any flu-like symptoms. Of course, most days my work schedule would require me to be there 12 hours a day, leaving my home at dawn and not returning until dusk, so I didn't recall communicating with her when she was awake for the past few days. At work, we pride ourselves on the fact that we had a lean management team, meaning very few individuals in top-tier leadership.

When we had visitors to the plant, as managers for the new continuous improvement department, we were required to host dinner meetings and attend many other after-work networking commitments. It was just one of our many job expectations. Granted, I loved whining and dining with our international guests and showing off our outstanding, state-of-the-art work as it was A+ level and new to the entire organization. Sadly, after looking back, the stress of multiple demands on my life was tough to handle, and something had to give.

"OH, BABY - I NEVER KNEW."

As I walked into the Nurse's office, I looked for her but saw no one. Then the counselor entered and walked me back to another area of the office. Some beds and curtains covered those who were resting. That's when she pulled one of the curtains back and I saw my beautiful child, 16 years young, having an anxiety attack. She was lying on her side, balled up in a fetal position. I tried to comfort her, but she told me to stay away and not to touch her. At first, I reacted like any parent would, and said, "Come on Mija, let's go home" and "Stop playing around, you're wasting people's time, now get up and let's go!" My voice became stern as I did not know what to do. I was in a "fight or flight" mode and all I wanted to do was fly away and take care of this in the privacy of our home. In the first place, it completely took me by surprise and secondly, I didn't understand what was happening. We were a very private family and keenly aware of how we were being perceived by our circle of family and friends. On that day they diagnosed her as having a panic attack but back in my day, it would have been referred to as a nervous breakdown. How do I know? Both my grandmother and mother had struggled with the same episodes.

Fast forward fourteen years, and knowing what I know now; we were doing it all wrong. At that time, just before my daughter's panic attack occurred, her schedule had changed drastically. I required much more from her and her older sibling than ever before. Now, you might be thinking I was only asking what any family would ask of their children, but it was the combination of changes that occurred that I believe was a major cause. These are my thoughts on what could have triggered the episode. My daughter suddenly became a part-time caregiver for both her youngest sibling and her grandmother because our beloved Melissa could no longer continue to assist us and needed to move back home. That meant my daughter was unable to continue her after-school sports or be involved in any other social activities for a while. In doing so, she was less active and more sedentary and her body felt the consequences. Fast food became our "go-to" staples with Chinese takeout, pizza, and mac and cheese as the top three favorites.

Let's compare the lifestyle suggestions from Brain Health experts that help to push back potential mental health problems, referred to as the *SIX to FIX* for optimal mental wellness to the drastic changes that were happening at the time:

1. Drink water, 60oz minimum. (Replaced by coffee).
2. Move daily, 30 minutes. (Removed sports).
3. Eat whole foods, limit sugar and processed foods.(Removed family gatherings for dinner).
4. Sleep at least 7 hours nightly. (Probably not, removed the supervision).
5. Take daily medication or supplements. (Not following any regimen).
6. Socialize. (Took away 90% of this option as she needed to be home more often).

Am I saying that it was all my fault, absolutely not. *Mamas only know what they know.* No guilt or condemnation here. I am simply sharing a pain so that you, my readers, can turn it around into a lesson. Learn from me, please.

Currently, mental health issues are on the rise in our society and have quadrupled since we officially moved into the post-pandemic era. The rise in new cases from teens and young adults is causing a rift in our culture as those who do not understand the condition often make insensitive and ignorant comments.

"The sad fact is that almost 8 million kids in the U.S. suffer from a mental health disorder,....Nearly one in six elementary children are affected by a mental health disorder. No matter if they are six or sixteen when a child asks for help, we must listen." Intermountainhealthcare.org

It is my observation, I feel that the Latino community still has a problem dealing with mental illness. As a family, we knew that our extended family members were not ready to understand our situation, so we kept a tight lid on the whole affair. She eventually graduated from high school and moved on to college away from us, far, far away from us. It wasn't an entire school year that went by when her mental health was, once again, an issue and we got the call. Because of the HIPPA laws regarding privacy for health-related issues, we never received notice about any medical concerns from the college. This time the call was from her roommate. They were both finishing up the Spring semester of college when Ely called, "Hi, it's Ely, you all might want to come and visit, she has not been out of the room for many weeks." This time it was much more severe. We had to do more intervention. Doctors, college counselors, therapists, and medicine had to be included in the recovery approach this time. She was able to finish off her semester well, with some adaptations, but either way, the family all woke up to the reality that this condition was going to be a constant priority for us all and that it was not going away any time soon.

At present, and into her 30s, she has managed to maintain an even keel with her brain health and has shared her experiences with teens and young adults by writing a fictional story with some true examples of her brain health challenges and triumphs in a book titled: Sea Glass, and Salt Air – Micaela Nicolini.

STIGMA THAT HURTS.

"She's what!?" asked a close family member when I finally decided to share the mental health challenges that we were going through. "You mean, she's crazy, are you sure she's not faking it?" I just wanted to cry, but instead, I got angry. How could they be so insensitive, I thought to myself. I could write pages and pages of situations that have come up regarding stigma-related comments and situations from that moment onwards, but this is not the time to go into that. All I ask is that you, my reader, think before you speak when it comes to talking about mental illness/brain health.

We all have causes that we get behind in our lives, animal rights, civil rights, women's rights, whatever that is for you, I say "more power to you" (power fist pump). This is my cause and my WHY. To understand what was going on in my daughter's brain, I decided to become a Licensed Brain Health Trainer for Dr. Daniel Amen M.D. of Amen Clinics. It is a license that allows me to teach his material to groups that are concerned with mental wellness. One of my most popular courses for workplace teams is *BrainFit for Work and Life*.

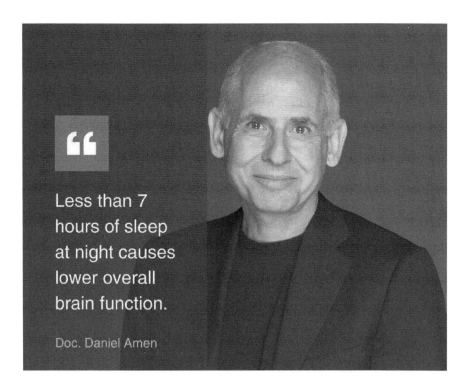

"

Less than 7 hours of sleep at night causes lower overall brain function.

Doc. Daniel Amen

Dr. Amen is a physician, adult and child psychiatrist, and founder of Amen Clinics with 11 locations across the U.S. Amen Clinics has the world's largest database of brain scans for psychiatry totaling more than 210,000 SPECT scans on patients from 155 countries. He is the founder of BrainMD, a fast-growing, science-based nutraceutical company, and Amen University, which has trained thousands of medical and mental health professionals in the methods he has developed. Dr. Daniel Amen's mission is to end mental illness by creating a revolution in brain health.

One day, I remember sharing with my daughter that I was interested in learning more about the brain, via a phone conversation. I said, "I have decided to follow the teachings of a brain expert, Dr. Daniel Amen of Amen Clinics because I want to learn how the brain works, you should look him up yourself." Her response was immediate, "Oh no, not another one of your 'Quack Doctors', No thank you!" I then encouraged her to just look him up and let me know what she thought. It wasn't until a few months later that I got a call from her, the voice on the other end was high-pitched in excitement, "Mama, I just looked up your Dr. Amen and I've got to say, he looks pretty LEGIT!" (That's short for legitimate).

"Thank you, Jesus!" I murmured under my voice. She began to investigate his method for treating brains and together we started with baby steps. From that point forward, I believe we began to speak the same brain health language. Has it been all peaches and cream since then? No. Just like weight loss, brain health is a journey. One very important element, that we have both learned, is instead of using the word "mental illness", we now refer to it as "brain health". Why? Because it is not an issue of the mind, it is a brain issue. A brain that is experiencing a chemical imbalance. We need to teach society, (that means each other), this simple statement,

"If the brain is not working well, our lives will not be working well".
– Dr. Daniel Amen, M.D.

So where do we start?

UNDERSTAND THE BASIC BRAIN BIOLOGY

"You are not stuck with the brain you have. There are steps you can take to make it function better." **– Dr. Caroline Leaf**, *Pathologist and Cognitive Neuroscientist*

The brain is made up of one billion neurons. It only weighs about 6 lbs and is housed in your skull which is made up of hard bony ridges on the inside. It is the consistency of butter or hard cream cheese. When thinking about the brain and its functions, note that there are four circles or systems that we must consider. Ask yourself, do I ever consider how I treat the four systems of my brain? My answer would have been, "NO!" Like most of us, we don't ever think of our brain as something that we could change.

THE FOUR CIRCLES OF HEALTH AND ILLNESS

The following represents four circles of physical and mental health that create a true balance. If one circle is off balance we are more likely to believe unhealthy thoughts.

» **Biological** – how the physical aspects of your brain and body function. This circle includes diet and exercise.
» **Psychological** – how you think and talk to yourself. Your self-concept, body image, emotional trauma, upbringing, and significant life events.
» **Social** – the quality of your relationships and any current life successes. With solid relationships comes a brain that functions better.
» **Spiritual** – your connection to God, the planet, and past and future generations; and your deepest sense of meaning and purpose.

Please see the handout to assist in fine-tuning your self-evaluation of the four circles of brain health at the end of the chapter.

Take some time to work through the examples of the four systems of the brain. To cultivate balance, you must be willing to work on one area of each system consistently. Read through each column and circle something that you feel is lacking in your life at the moment. Then make a plan to begin to challenge yourself in that area.

IF, THEN

"If you have a crushing chest pain, your doctor will scan your heart; but if you have a crushing depression. No one will ever look at your brain.

If you are sick to your stomach, your doctor will image your abdomen; but if you are sick with anxiety, no one will ever look at your brain.

If you have stabbing back pain, your doctor will order an MRI; but if you have urges to stab others, no one will ever look at your brain.

If you have persistent knee pain, your doctor will image your knees; but if you have persistent heartache, no one will ever look at your brain.

If you have a chronic cough, your doctor will x-ray your chest; if alcoholic behavior is ruining your life, no one will ever look at your brain.

If you have tormenting hip pain, your doctor will scan your hip; but if you torment your spouse so much that he or she leaves you, no one will ever look at your brain".

The End of Mental Illness
– Dr. Daniel Amen, M.D.

OUR AWESOME, BONITA BRAIN

"Mama, I have some news and you might want to sit down to hear this", said my daughter. I automatically thought to myself, she's pregnant. So, I sat down and immediately felt nervous feelings deep in my stomach. "I have been diagnosed with bipolar disorder level 2 and I brought some books so that you can read up on this condition. As a "Doer", at the time, I was involved in a hundred different projects. I had a ton of items on my things-to-do list and needed to stop my momentum and just focus on what my daughter had shared with me. Therefore, I went into "fix-it" mode and responded, "Okay, so what do we do next? Is there a pill or something that you can take to get better?" I am ashamed to say it but, I kept this update between just the three of us, her dad, myself, and her. I wanted to be able to address what was happening before I shared it with the rest of the family. It took several years before I actually opened those books that she had given me as I knew that if she just

_____, fill in the blank, it would go away. No, that was wrong.

As I close this chapter, let's be clear on something crucially important. Psychiatric issues are so much more complicated than the average layperson has considered, that includes me. They have evolved from inhumane treatment in the 14th century to the 15-minute check-in with a Physician's Assistant, today.   In a society where we say, "Just give me a pill and let me be on my way" we have so much work to do in this area.

As an individual, we must make this invisible illness visible by talking about it openly and striving for optimal brain health.

As a society, we need to shift away from how we see mental illness and begin using the word "Brain Health" instead.   Remember your brain creates what your mind fixates on.

Knowing this information has strengthened our relationship. I now understand what was happening to my precious adult child. And no, she wasn't faking it!

MEDICAL DISCLAIMER

The information presented in this book is the result of years of practical experience and clinical research by Dr. Daniel Amen, M.D. The information is presented by a Licensed Brain Health Trainer with Amen Clinics and is of a general nature and not a substitute for an evaluation or treatment by a competent medical specialist. If you believe that you need medical intervention, *please see a medical practitioner as soon as possible.*

BIOLOGICAL	PSYCHOLOGICAL	SOCIAL	SPIRITUAL
Athleticism	Authenticity	Caring	Acceptance
Beauty	Confidence	Connection	Appreciation
Brain Health	Courage	Dependability	Awareness (Awe)
Energy	Creativity	Empathy	Compassion
Focus	Flexibility	Encouragement	Generosity
Fitness	Forthrightness	Family	Gratitude
Longevity	Fun	Friendships	Growth
Love - Brain/Body	Happiness/Joy	Independence	Humility
Mental clarity	Hard work	Kindness	Inspiration
Physical health	Individuality	Love of others	Love/relationship w/God
Safety	Love-self	Loyalty	Morality
Strength	Open-minded	Outcome driven/service	Patience
Vitality	Positivity	Passion	Prayerful
	Resilience	Significance	Purposeful
	Responsibility	Success	Religious community
	Science-based	Tradition	Surrender
	Security		Transcendence
	Self-control		Wonder

five

OUR THOUGHTS LIE! HELLO AWESOME BRAIN

"Whatever we plant in our minds and nourish with repetition and emotion will one day become our reality" **– Earl Nightingale**

My history with the subject of brain health goes much deeper than what I have already shared. Not so much regarding the academia of brain functions, but in being a member of a family with a history of brain health issues. Writing on this subject required me to conjure up some of the most emotionally taxing and deeply personal feelings that, in all transparency, have been buried since long ago. On the days when I would sit and write a few more paragraphs to add to this chapter, I'd literally have to take a nap afterward and would often feel emotionally drained for the remainder of my day. But enough about that, let's discuss the biology of our awesome brain.

During the pre-World War I era, it was common to hear terms like, "Crippled", "Retarded", "Insane", "Socially Defective", and "Lunatic" to describe those in our society who were disabled or suffering from mental illness. At present we now use the term "special needs" and it seems much more humane. The history of treatment for their conditions and opportunities for inclusion into society has gone from revoltingly inhumane to hopeful. I am thankful that we have evolved to this point in our society and that I live in the 21st Century, but there is so much more we need to do, and certainly, we are just scratching the surface of understanding the needs of those who suffer.

The opportunity to learn about the brain and its functions has shown me a clearer picture of life and a deeper connection to explaining many of life's challenges. Knowing what I do about the awesome functions of the brain has changed my perception, and helped me to answer my why. The brain is a vastly intricate organ, and we now know that everything we do begins with the brain. How does one even begin to tackle this subject? Well here goes!

THE AWESOME BRAIN

Do you remember the "awesome" phase of communicating with one another? Everything was described in that manner. I think it was introduced during the surfer era. "You look awesome, man!" "That experience was awesome!" "That person spoke in such an awesome way!" I remember using that term to retell an experience and the receiver replied to my story most unexpectedly, saying, "You know that term "awesome" has become so casual these days, we really aren't using it properly". I stopped and thought, first, of how rude he was for stopping me mid-sentence, and then second, how dare he try to give me a word syntax lesson. I chose not to react but responded with, "I see your point" and then moved on. Later that day, however, I was prompted to look the word up. Wikipedia gives this definition: *"Awesome is defined as causing or inducing awe, inspiring an overwhelming feeling of reverence, admiration or fear"*. From this definition, the word "reverence" seemed to jump out at me as I thought, "Reverence?" Really? I save the word reverence for the action of getting on my knees and worshiping God, or something.

As I speak of the brain for the remainder of this book, I want you to know that I am fully aware of its power to shape our lives. If you are willing and ready to listen and act, your life could change for the better. Furthermore, I will be using the term, "awesome" with a full understanding of its original meaning and I am wholeheartedly in agreement with the definition.

SMALL BUT MIGHTY

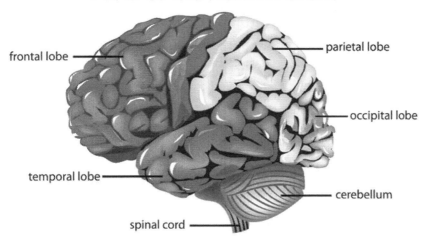

Parts of the Human Brain

I now recognize the brain to be the most intricate and awesome organ in the body. According to Dr. Daniel Amen, M.D., Neuroscientist and creator of the Brain SPECT Scan, the brain has one billion neurons, weighs about 6lbs, requires 20% to 30% of your daily caloric intake to function well, which includes fats, and is the consistency of butter or firm cream cheese. It is housed in your skull; The skull is made up of a hard surface of bony ridges on the top underside, therefore abrupt movements like jerking or shaking can and does cause trauma to your brain. It needs H2O to function well, therefore, clear, clean water is crucial to brain health. To take that even further, for every pound you weigh, you need to drink half an ounce of water daily to maintain optimal health for your organs, which includes the brain. For instance, if I weigh 160 lbs., then I need to drink 80 ounces of water a day just to keep my organs functioning well. Let me be clear, water means water and does not imply any other type of liquid. In other words, four giant 20 oz servings of coffee at a time do not meet the water requirements for the 80 oz just described. Let me continue to be a "bummer" to you all by stating that any drink that is caffeinated actually subtracts from your hydration requirements. The brain's main source of energy is achieved through sleep; Lovely, amazing sleep. There is sleep and there is real sleep. Sleeping on the couch while bingeing Netflix is not quality sleep because you never reach Rapid Eye Movement, or REM. REM sleep is attained when one sleeps deeply and is in a dream state of mind for a long period. Sleep is so important to the health of our bodies that it directs a circadian flush to happen throughout this time of required rest. This flush is a way to cleanse the body's organs and requires at least 7 hours, at minimum, to complete.

A fun fact and interesting observation states that the brain can hold the capacity of information equivalent to six million years of a daily subscription to the Wall Street Journal.

In essence, our society is walking around dehydrated to a dangerous degree. And, if our 7 hours of sleep minimum has not been achieved, then what do we do? Get COFFEE, the stronger the better. So, what if you find yourself experiencing the dreaded "mid-day slump"? More COFFEE! Can you see where I'm going here? It's like we're all hamsters on a wheel, spinning round and round and thinking that we are doing well for ourselves. By not practicing the basic behaviors that our brain needs to function well, we continue to mistreat it and wonder why we can't move forward. More on this topic later as I don't want to discourage you at this point. The last thing I want is for you to put the book down and never come back to finish it.

Now, can you understand why I felt intimidated by this subject? I have spent six years wrestling with a strong desire to write about it and the last two years intensely researching brain health; finally, I feel worthy of sharing what I have learned. Why? you may ask. The answer is clear because I know someone will benefit from this information. I pray that someone is you!

"The secret to overcoming anxiety, both now and for the rest of your life, is to work on optimizing the physical functioning of your brain."
– Dr. Daniel Amen, M.D.

Dear Mama, I get it now...

"DEAR MAMA, I GET IT NOW!"

It was 1948 and she was just 16 years old. Which for many teenagers is a year of exploration and excitement for life. She was a spry young lady, living her best life in San Francisco, California, also known as "The

City". Anyone who has lived in California for any length of time knows that reference, just like when you talk about the University of California college system and its many school campuses; however, the first one, UC Berkeley, was built in 1868 and is often referred to simply as: "Cal".

Mama, her parents, and her six siblings lived in an area of San Francisco known as the Mission District. A sprawling urban development where new transplants to the city gravitated. An Influx of young Latino families, specifically Mexican-Americans, from the State of Texas were recruited to work in the shipyards in support of the war efforts. Mama and her family arrived from Aransas Pass Texas, a small town near Corpus Christi. My grandfather acquired a job as a "Slinger ", a person who would hurl long cables from one part of the ship to the other. My grandfather was very fit and stood over 6 feet tall. The job was not an easy one and was potentially life-threatening as one could easily fall into the open water, but his size and physical abilities kept him prepared to tackle the job requirements.

After reading much about the women of the war efforts, I recall that my eldest Aunt was considered to be a "Rosie the Riveter". In short, Rosie the Riveter was a cultural icon in the USA that represented women who left their domestic lifestyles to work in factories and shipyards during WWII, mainly to assemble tools and such. A woman wearing a polka-dotted red handkerchief on her head and posing while wearing a man's work shirt and flexing her arm muscles is the iconic image of Rosie the Riveter, and that was my Tia Delia.

Mama was attending high school at the time and getting ready to enjoy a "Sock Hop" the following Friday. She was extra excited to be able to be around her friends. On this day, once school was over, as she did every day, she hopped onto the school bus and was on her route home. Looking out the window Mama was daydreaming about the outfit she had recently purchased for the dance, she loved to dance. The outfit was a baby blue flowy skirt with sparkling silver sequence and a white button-up cardigan sweater with a short blue scarf she would wear around her neck. She was awakened from her trance by the sounds of a group of friends walking along the sidewalk going in the opposite direction. Quickly, she stuck her head out of the school bus window and yelled, "Hello". They noticed her and said "Hi" back and proceeded to invite her to come along with them to Woolworth's for an ice cream. Woolworth's was an Ice Cream/Soda Shop and department store. It was known for its walk-up counter service and many young adults would frequent it after the school day was out. She couldn't resist the invitation and asked the bus driver to let her off at the upcoming intersection or anywhere there was an opportunity to stop. The bus was driving Southbound. When allowed, she jumped off the bus and waited at the intersection for an "all-clear" sign from her friends who were watching and waving her over from across the busy street. Cars were passing quickly in front of her so it took her a few tries before she attempted to cross the street.

It was a cold Spring afternoon. The day had been overcast and had just begun to clear. The sun was starting to peek through the clouds, which was a common climate for The City by the Bay. Most residents knew to dress in layered clothing for that reason, it was cloudy in the morning and a bit more sunny in the late afternoon. My mother was a stylish young lady and often wore fashionable clothing to school, more so as she got older and began doing odd jobs for the neighbors to make the funds that were required to look fashionable. She had a talent for ironing and would often get requests from women in her neighborhood who knew of the financial status of her family. It brought in a few dollars a month and she saved every one of them for shopping opportunities with friends.

On this day she was wearing a pink wool overcoat with large, padded shoulders. Looking both to her right and to her left, she stepped out onto the street to cross it quickly. What happened next was told to me in bits and pieces as it was not something Mama desired to remember, whether suppressed or because of some other brain issues, the remainder of the story simply stops there. She did share that she thought the "coast was clear", so she darted out and a car came around the corner at high speed and caught her coat on the rearview mirror by the shoulder pad. She recounts that she didn't think she screamed and that she may have just been knocked unconscious as the driver continued to drive, not recognizing that she was being dragged.

The cars of the 1940s were "big tank" looking models, and I have always known them as "Bombs". They were constructed of heavy steel with smaller windows and not at all like those constructed in the 21st Century. Mama's friends were watching everything as it was happening and when they saw her being hit, proceeded to let out a series of screams, waving down the driver to stop. Of course, they were standing on the other side of the busy intersection and were not easily noticed.

Next, she remembers waking up in the hospital. Three days later, after several days in a coma and many surgeries. In a matter of seconds, she went from a "normal" teenager to a disabled girl who became a "burden to society", (her words not mine); a society that was just learning how to handle the rights of women, Black Americans, and the disabled, specifically, those with mental illness.

Children: 1900-1945 who needed physical assistance were often referred to as crippled. Depending on the severity of their health issues, for educational purposes, they were housed together, often in single rooms and separated from the mainstream of other students. Eventually, they would be trained as low-skilled workers at best.

YOUTUBE VIDEO EARLY EDUCATION FOR THE DISABLED

Our society was just learning how to handle those children with special needs and there was much trial, and error cited in our history about that time. Depression, anxiety disorders, concussions, and disability or deformities in children and adults, were often dealt with inhumanely. Specifically, there were Lunatic Hospitals and Insane Asylums for the mentally ill and those with physical and mental conditions. If you were one of those who suffered from an anxiety disorder or depression you could expect the following treatment: insulin injections, lobotomy, and electric shock. I shudder at the thought that my loved ones would have been subjected to those medical remedies. That is why we need to continue to talk about brain health and about the many ways to address it humanely. To fully understand the history of treatment for those with mental health issues, see the chart at the end of the chapter entitled, A Brief History of Mental Health Treatment.

In the 1940s, when my mother was just a child, there were no real signs of improvements in the benevolent treatment of the disabled. Children were oftentimes removed from society and hidden from the general public.

For the next decade, my grandparents would quite literally control her every move and wait on her "hand and foot". She never cooked or cleaned or had responsibility for any chores as she was now considered "La Pobresita", (the poor little girl). After being released from the hospital, she was transferred away from the school and friends that she absolutely loved and moved to a one-room schoolhouse on the outskirts of San Francisco named, ironically enough, SUNSHINE School for the Disabled. It was anything but that. It was a catch-all school that housed all children from the ages of 5 to 18 years who were considered "Special Needs". Twelve months passed and it was all that Mama could take from that school environment, so she soon dropped out. She eventually returned to school in her late 40s, as a re-entry student, and earned her high school diploma from her original high school in the Mission District of San Francisco.

I recall her response to being asked why she didn't just finish school at the Sunshine School. She responded abruptly and said, "I suddenly had to spend the entire day with children of all ages and varying degrees of disabilities. Kids with trach tubes inserted into their throats and others without legs and others who would cry out in what seemed, to me, to be pain, all day long, it scared the wits out of me!" She went on to say that she tried to help, but soon became depressed and could not think or concentrate well. All she wanted to do was go home. Her permanent disabilities would include her left arm never functioning well from that day forward. She had no control of it. It was limp and had very little circulation, even to the point that it was a dark red, almost blue color and she could only feel very little sensation. Oftentimes, it required me to let her know there was a wound or a cut on her arm. Most of the time she was not aware. Once she broke the bone and it healed incorrectly. The doctors often encouraged her to have her arm amputated, but she would never hear of it and honestly feared that it would be done without her consent. Her left leg was in bad shape as well and took on a different look as it was the primary location of many skin grafts to other areas of her body. Eventually, she would learn how to walk again. And, walking she did. Once she reached the age of independence, she was off! And would learn about life through much trial and error. I am not sure if my mother ever received any brain health medical intervention of any kind. I didn't know about this information before she passed on, or I would have asked. Knowing the history of mental health treatments, as I do now, I think not. Looking back, it's all a "Would'a Could'a Should'a" time for me.

ONE TOUGH COOKIE

I think the more my grandparents, mostly my grandfather, would hover over her and try and control her every move, the more my mother would wiggle out of that grip and long to be her 16-year-old self again.

At 22 years old, she became pregnant and had my eldest brother, at 24 another brother, at 26 another brother, and then at 28 years, her #1 blessing from above was born, ME! Finally, as her last hurrah, my sister was born 9.5 years later at age 38. She was a disabled, single parent of five children with "drop-in daddies" who paid some child support, from time to time, and others who, to this day, will not acknowledge their children. Despite all that, she soldiered on.

As we journeyed together, my mother and I, and she was well into her late 70s, I remember someone asking her about how she became disabled; she would begin to describe her past and, just for fun, I would often interject, when appropriate of course, and say, "Excuse me but don't let her fool you into thinking she is disabled." I'd continue by saying, "You weren't *THAT* disabled because you managed to make 5 babies, from 3 baby daddies, somehow." She'd always let out a huge laugh and respond with, "Ay Mija, don't say that about your Mama." She never married one of them, and to this day, I don't know who was against marriage, her or them, but I know she always taught me never to let a man control me. Did her words settle deep into my subconscious? Oh yes, and they could have derailed me many times in my marriage, but we hung on. I'm proud to say, I am currently working on my 41st year of marriage to the love of my life.

I think back, "How in the heck did my siblings and I make it?" I think that's why we stayed so close to each other because we needed to band together. I say again, "Thank you, God, you get all the glory, here."

Why would you thank God? Your home life was a mess, you might say. My rebuttal would be, but we were all allowed to be here! At the time when Mama was in her 20s & 30s birth control pills and other forms of family planning options were just gathering popularity. The Women's Liberation Movement was in full swing and honestly, although it wasn't common, my mother could have had every justification for terminating every one of her pregnancies. No judgment or condemnation for those of my readers who choose those options, as we are talking about my mother's case here. I thank God for the opportunity to have been born and, every day on my birthday, I would make it a point to contact her by telephone and thank her for having me. It was guaranteed to begin the "waterworks" as she would say. She would cry and I would sing her a Thank You to the tune of Happy Birthday.

At its worst, and most ignorant dealings of those with disabilities, I learned and am personally sickened by the term, Eugenics. It is an ancient method to deal with societies of unwanted people. It is a form of selective breeding and management for the genetic quality of the human population which states:

"Eugenics is a set of beliefs and practices that aim to improve the genetic quality of a human population, historically by excluding people and groups judged to be inferior and promoting those judged to be superior. The concept

predates the term; Plato suggested applying the principles of selective breeding to humans around 400 BC." Philosophyforlife.org

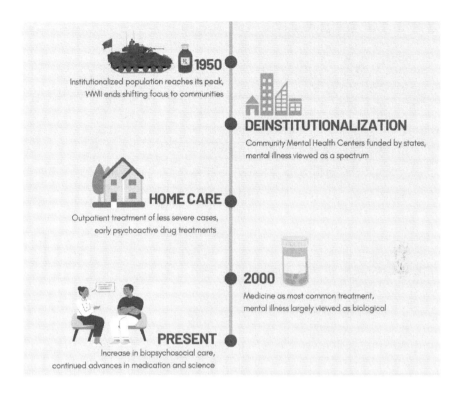

In regards to advancements in mental and physical health treatments and an impartial side note, here are some of the grand advancements in American laws that were established during my mother's developmental years, just to name a few:

» The Social Security Act of 1935
» Brown v. Board of Education Act, 1954
» Civil Rights Movement of the 1960s
» IDEA Individual Disability Education Act 1975
» Mills v Board of Education Act, 1975
» Americans with Disabilities Act, 1990

History and Philosophy of the Disability Rights Movement

MOST OF OUR THOUGHTS ARE BIG LIARS!

I was taught later on in my life that F.E.A.R. was an acronym for False Evidence Appearing Real. My Mama was taught to fear life, and rightly so, with the status of treatment for the disabled being as it was during her formative years. All she wanted to do was to embrace life. Maybe not at the beginning of her life but definitely by the end, she knew that society valued her as a person. A very intelligent, sober, contributor to this world, with or without sufficiently working body parts. Mama did the best she could to live a "normal life" and she will forever be a great example of a warrior and a great Mama.

GET YOUR THOUGHTS TOGETHER!

Stepping out to write this book after six years of preparation was the hardest part of this process. I know now that I would avoid it by being too busy, or should I say making excuses of being too busy. It wasn't

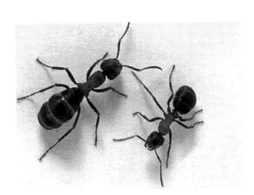

until I read the theory coined by Dr. Amen M.D. about the way our brains work and how we tend to gravitate to *automatic negative thoughts*. The acronym for this tendency is referred to as having ANTs. In his book, *Your Brain is Always Listening*, he describes this in more detail. Here are nine examples of the ANTs that we let infiltrate our minds. I was dealing with #2, Less Than ANT, and needed something to shift me out of that negative mindset.

1. All or Nothing ANTs: Thinking that things are either all good or all bad
2. Less-Than ANTs: Comparing or seeing yourself as less than others
3. Just-the-Bad ANTs: Seeing only the bad in a situation
4. Guilt-Beating ANTs: Thinking in words like should, must, ought, or have to
5. Labeling ANTs: Attaching a negative label to yourself or someone else
6. Fortune-Telling ANTs: Predicting the worst possible outcome for a situation with little or no evidence for it
7. Mind-ReadingANTs: Believing you know what other people are thinking even though they haven't told you
8. If-Only and I'll-Be-Happy-When ANTs: Arguing with the past and longing for the future
9. Blaming ANTs: Blaming someone else for your problems

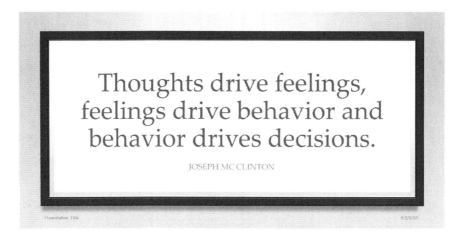

"A thought is harmless unless we believe it. It's not our thoughts, but the attachment to our thoughts, that causes suffering. Attaching to a thought means believing that it's true without inquiring. A belief is a thought that we've been attached to, often for years." **–Byron Katie**
Loving What Is: Four Questions that Can Change Your Life

FINAL NOTE:

Today, I learned of the passing of a very famous contemporary Christian artist. Her name was Mandisa, she was just 47 and was known for her endearing songs that gave hope to all who struggled with mental health and self-worth issues. She was outward and open about her struggles and often used her musical platform to speak to her fans. Here are the lyrics from one of my favorite singles entitled, *The Truth About Me*. It is a very fitting song and aligned with this chapter's topic. I was in the process of writing when I heard the news.

"The Truth About Me" - **Mandisa**

If only I could see me as you see me
And understand the way that I am loved
Would it give a whole new meaning to my purpose
Change the way I see the world
Would I sparkle like a star in the night sky?
Would I give a little more instead of take?
If I understood I'm precious like the diamond
I'm a worth no one could estimate
I'm a worth no one could estimate

[Chorus]
You say lovely
I say broken
I say guilty
You say forgiven
I feel lonely
Say you're with me
We both know it would change everything
If only I believed the truth about me

[Verse 2]
I wish I could hold on to the moments
When my life is spinnin but I'm peaceful still
Like a wind you whispered in the silence
And tell me things this world never will
You tell me things this world never will

[Chorus]
You say lovely
I say broken
I say guilty
You say forgiven
I feel lonely
Say you're with me
We both know it would change everything
If only I believed the truth about me

[Bridge]
I would sleep better at night
Wake up with hope for another day
I would love even if it cost me
Take a chance and know I'm goin be ok
I would dare to give my life away.

[Chorus]
Oh, I feel lonely
Say you're with me
We both know it would change everything
If only I believed the truth about me
If only I believed the truth about me

Tell your story.
Shout it. Write it.
Whisper it if you have to.
But tell it.
Some won't understand it.
Some will outright reject it.
But many will
thank you for it.
And then the most
magical thing will happen.
One by one, voices will start
whispering, 'Me, too.'
And your tribe will gather.
And you will never
feel alone again.

— L.R. Knost

six

MEXICO LINDO AND GOD BLESS AMERICA: THE PARADOX OF "AND"

"Until you make the unconscious conscious, it will direct your life and you will call it fate." **– Carl Jung**

I would be remiss if I did not dedicate some portion of the book to a deeper dive into my cultural background and societal struggles because of who I am; a female, Christian, wife of 41 years, mother of 3 amazing adult children, and Mexican American who is proud of both cultures. I may have given a hint into this position by incorporating a bit of "Spanglish", (Spanish and English), into the title. As a second-generation Mexican American, my mother was strongly encouraged to assimilate 100% percent to the "American ways" and she tried, but I ask you, "How do you do that exactly?" I was raised with cousins who were of mixed race, twenty-eight in total, from seven aunts and uncles including my mother. Some of my cousins were half Italian, half Filipino, and some were half White. Whenever we'd get together for family reunions and such, we'd seem to gravitate to our Mexican heritage. My grandparents were bilingual for the most part. My grandfather's primary language was English, and he could speak it without a trace of a Spanish accent, even though his first language was Spanish. Our grandmother could speak only a handful of English words and only really communicated in Spanish. She never received a formal education. My mother shared that after being born, our grandmother suffered severe postpartum depression and didn't speak much at all. You would often find her cupping her hands to her mouth and speaking softly into them in prayer. Her health eventually improved, but she never really developed her English language skills. Oh, but she tried!

MALCRIADOS!!

Speaking of my grandmother and her attempts to learn English reminds me of a time when she was eagerly practicing. I noticed children's books on the subject of the alphabet and phonetics on her nightstand. I remember she would carry a small chalkboard to copy letters onto it. She would then trace them with her finger and sound them out. Mind you, Grandma Frances was illiterate in both English and Spanish, so she was starting from ground zero. My brothers and I were there with her that day and we were intrigued to help her. Those brothers of mine were not at all what you would call "well-behaved". They were pranksters and in Spanish, we would call them Malcriados, (Brats). One day I caught them instructing my grandmother to write her letters on her chalkboard, telling her it would spell her name. They were very encouraging and patient with her and that was my first clue that they were up to no good. Upon closer inspection, I could see my grandmother looking encouraged and happy to be working with her grandsons. My first thought was, "Awe, that's nice of them." Then I looked at the chalkboard and the letters they were having her trace actually spelled, @ U C K Y O U! I immediately grabbed the board out of her hands and erased the letters telling her that they were wrong and that it did not spell her name and that she should forget it. Afterward, they swiftly ran away, howling in laughter. I still remember it to this day! The Malcriados' deny it to this day.

My point here is that we were told to assimilate into our Country, the USA, and we are proud to be Americans. After all, many of our Mexican-American family members fought in several American wars to defend our American freedoms and liberties, but if you would have asked any of us to communicate a sentence in Spanish to one another, then, you'd probably get blank stares and shoulder shrugs, for certain! Furthermore, we knew nothing about Mexico. There's a name for people like me and the majority of my relatives.

I keep up with social media updates and trends via my youngest son. He is an Influencer in his mid-20s and often shares the new terms or trends with me. It's mostly for comedic purposes as I think he loves seeing how I react. I was sharing with him my struggle to write this chapter, specifically the conflict of the "And/Or Paradox". The loyalty to two cultures but one pride. I talked with my son about the youth not knowing a thing about Mexico but celebrating all that is Mexican. He responded, "Oh, you mean the 'No-Sabo' Kids?" I choked on my response and asked, "What?" He continued by saying, "Yup, that's the new word for the youth that are SUPER Whitewashed." He explained that social media has categorized them to be brown kids that have no clue about their heritage, hence the "NO-Sabo" (don't know) kids. He went on to say, "They are the first ones to get in line for their margaritas on Cinco de Mayo and shout a loud "Ole!" but have no clue why they are doing it." I just had to laugh. Mostly, because he was talking about himself and his siblings.

Nevertheless, I was taught to be proud of my heritage, whether it was intentional or not. The focus at social events was always Mexican food and music, and the language was primarily Spanish. The message was, God Bless America, and Viva Mexico Lindo (Beautiful), and that was our paradox. I saw it as a contradiction. How could "they" want me to be loyal to the two entities? You see I understood it to be an either-OR situation. I soon learned that it was an AND.

"Paradox is not an emotion…it starts with thinking but brings in emotion as we start to feel the tension and pull of different ideas…we need to allow the seeming contradictions to coexist to gain a deeper understanding. Paradoxes force us to think in expansive ways and lean into vulnerability."
Atlas of the Heart - **Brene Brown**

THE ULTIMATUM

Sitting pretty in a job that I felt perfectly prepared for and feeling like I had arrived at heights unexpected in my career, I was on my way to meet with the Vice Chancellor of the university. Having recently married and in my early 20s, I was very excited to be working as the Student

Services Coordinator II for the University of California, Berkeley. My job required that I go into high schools and encourage students from low-income and marginalized areas in the Bay Area to consider the UC system as an option for higher education. The problem, at the time, was the UC system had the highest and most rigorous requirements for admissions. Most who intended on arriving at admission considerations in their senior year of high school would have had to begin preparing as early as elementary school, 6th grade, to be exact. That was, in a nutshell, my task, to go out into the inner cities and the rural farming communities and share the advantages of early educational and financial planning for college, some six years away.

Meeting with school counselors and other administrators allowed for an avenue into the lives of the students. Once the presentations were over and I was able to talk with the students one-on-one, it was guaranteed they would end up saying, "I don't think my parents will let me go because even if I did meet the requirements, we wouldn't have the money, so why should I even worry about it?"

As previously mentioned, my mother's mantra was always, "Education is our Freedom", and after working for the UC system, (UC Berkeley and UC Santa Barbara), I realized that, truly, it was. It was another paradox and this time my challenge was to convince the students to try. As I strategized my approach, I knew that I had to get the parents involved. After all, once they were supportive of higher education, my job would be smooth sailing. One problem, most of the parents in my recruitment area spoke only Spanish, and though I wasn't a "No Sabo" kid, I surely wasn't fluent enough to present the benefits of college life to the parents in a bilingual fashion.

"We are modifying our recruitment approach to include parents from all service regions, and we need you to present the college message in Spanish, can you do that?" said Vice Chancellor Hernandez. Suddenly, I felt nauseous, my eyes widened, and a rush of sweat beads began to form on my face. "I can certainly understand Spanish, and maybe even get by with a few sentences here and there, but I am not comfortable presenting an entire presentation in Spanish," I replied. "Well, that's what we need, I suggest you do what you can to get ready, take night classes and we'll pay for the tuition as a professional development benefit. Do this ASAP or we'll have to begin looking for someone else." He said and walked away.

Fast forward to the arrangement; I would have a year to become fully bilingual in occupational Spanish, meaning for work-related communication at minimum. After two semesters of taking night school classes at the local community college, it was suggested that I immerse myself in the Spanish language by spending some time in Mexico. As a result, I used most of my month's worth of vacation time to go live with a host family to attend IDEAL - Instituto de Estudios America-Latino. My childhood buddy, Chill, was a school counselor at the time and had Summers' off, so she joined me.

Food is all about flavor, (Sabor). But there are so many layers to what and why we eat, boredom, depression, association with comfort, and oh yes, hunger. We use food as a crutch and are socialized to eat to be included. But there is an awakening that happens when you travel outside your country, your state, your community, and your comfort zone. I was about to become awakened to Mexican culinary delights that would change the way I understood the food of my upbringing.

IMMERSION INTO A CULTURE, I NEVER REALLY KNEW.

Knowing, now, what I do about my Mexican roots, a huge misconception about food was cleared up during the stay with my host family in this foreign country. I thought that all Mexicans had the same flavor palette and that we, in America, mimicked how they eat in their country. Let me help you understand where I am going with this by sharing a day in the life of an IDEAL student:

SCHEDULE FOR IDEAL SCHOOL
REPEATED DAILY

Monday through Friday

» 6:00 am – 6:30 am Rise and Shine/Get Ready

» 6:45 am – 7:15 am Breakfast

  / Water

  / Canela Tea (Cinnamon), not coffee

  / Melba Toast, no butter

  / Scrambled eggs from the chickens at residence (or, prepared as you choose)

  / Melon or other choice fruits, (fresh) from their garden

» 7:30 am – 8:00 am Walk to School campus (1 mile)

  / One mile to the campus, (all uphill) on our way there.

» 8:15 am – 10:00 am First Class

» 10:00 am – 10:15 am Break

  / Mango or Pineapple on a stick, small servings

  / Nuts, packaged almonds, or peanut

  / Water

» 10:15 am – 12:00 pm Second Class

» 12:00 pm – 2:30 pm Siesta (Afternoon rest time)

  / Walk home, eat lunch, rest - This was our main meal of the day. (1 mile)

    › Fresh black beans (not pinto beans)

> › Grilled protein, (Fish or chicken, weekends was beef)
> › Salsa
> › White rice, not covered in red sauce, and topped with mixed vegetables
> › Vegetables (cooked or grilled)
> › Handmade corn tortillas (no white flour)
> › Queso fresco - fresh cheese (sprinkle, not floating over the top of the food)

» 2:30 pm – 3:00 pm Walk back to the campus uphill (1 Mile)

» 3:10 pm – 4:40 pm Third Class

» 4:40 pm - 6:30 pm – Spanish language conversation/Homework/Tutoring opportunities

» 6:30 pm – 7:00 pm – Walk Home (1 Mile)

» 7:30 pm – 8:00 pm Light Dinner
> / Toast and Tea, and/or Yogurt

» 8:00 pm – 9:00 pm Open Time (TV Spanish language only, strictly enforced)

» 9:00 pm - Lights out!

Weekends

Saturday – Drove to the market and went to a pastry shop, and movie theater, and shopped for pleasure. No English was ever allowed, but I believe we snuck some in from time to time.

Sunday – Rest, go to church, if you decided to, yet it was not required, and prepare for the upcoming week.

While walking home for lunch, I mentioned to Chill that I was especially hungry. I told her that I was ready to devour my mid-day meal. When we arrived at the host home, I could smell the food as it was being fried outside in their courtyard in a huge wok. It smelled delicious. As we sat down to eat, we began to dig right into the meal and as I usually did, I tasted everything and proceeded to compliment the chef. The chicken was especially tasty. I named all the items on my plate in Spanish and was almost 100% accurate until I came to the name of the protein dish. I asked, "Pollo, Si Senora?" The reply was "NO". I continued to think of another word for chicken and asked "Pavo?" And again, the response was still, No. In my best broken Spanish, I said, "Que tipo de comida es?"(What type of food is this?)She replied, Paloma. " I replied, "No te intiendo." (I don't understand you?) Then she pointed outside at the pigeons on the window sill and said, "Paloma", with a frustrated tone in her voice. You guessed it! I was eating pigeons and apparently, they were considered a high-priced delicacy that was made especially for her most cherished guests. I gladly finished up the rest of the food on the plate but left what remained of the pigeon. I just couldn't do it. I kept looking out of the window and thinking, "Those poor birdies." That evening Chill warned me that it was rude to criticize the food that we were served by our host family and that we needed to be careful as we were paid guests, but guests, nonetheless. As Chill and I lay in bed that evening we began to reminisce about how different our lives were back in the States. I asked, "Chill, what would you wish for right now if you could have anything?", she responded, "Anything? That's a lot to think about but honestly, I'd wish for a big fat

QUARTER POUNDER with cheese!" After letting out a loud rant of laughter, I replied, "Oh you're so bad". I then shared my wish, "I wish I had unlimited amounts of chicken McNuggets and BBQ sauce and I do mean chicken, not PIGEON!" We continued to howl in laughter with pillows over our faces like young schoolgirls. I guess that's what we were. Without fail, we heard a loud knock on our door and the Dona de la casa (ma'am) of the house shouted out, NO INGLES! We were forbidden to speak, read, hear, or write anything in English. Today, I still believe in total immersion when trying to learn a second language. It worked for me, and I wouldn't change a thing.

During my time in Mexico, I most definitely learned that one or the other is better than both of anything regarding food. Our mentality shifted as our menu was limited and choices were few. In hindsight, the "OR" was our lesson. We needed to sleep well *OR* we'd be very tired that following day and learning a foreign language was much more challenging brain work than we ever thought before.

Life is a paradox as we often get ourselves into trouble by having too many choices. Adopting the "AND", that's to say, "I want this and that and also some of that" is not profitable for optimum brain health. During my time in Mexico, I learned that if we are serious about our health and wellness, healthy decisions must be made and, in this instance, that requires us to choose the "OR".

Let's look at the benefits of this school schedule and filter it through what Dr. Amen suggests we do to optimize our brain health. For more information, please see chapter Four *"The Bonita Brain"*. To recap the happy brain moves, we're advised to incorporate the following six actions into our lives daily to maximize our brain health, they are the SIX to FIX:

Requirements	Mexico Schedule
Drink water, 60oz minimum.	Drank water all day
Move daily, 30 minutes.	Walked 4 miles daily
Eat whole foods, limit sugar and processed foods.	Nothing we ate was
processed, some sugar on the weekends during our one day out at the	
neighborhood market.	
Sleep at least 7 hours nightly.	Schedule dictated 8 hours
Take daily medication or supplements.	No regimen on this
Socialize.	Yes, often

After some time, I did learn to speak, read, and write Spanish much more fluently, and was able to meet some great people in the process. I learned that Mexico was a beautiful country with so much history and a rich vibrant culture, the history of my ancestors. I learned that what we consider "Mexican food" in the US, is not common within the neighborhoods we frequented in Mexico.

I returned to work, after several weeks, more equipped to work with the parents who needed the information shared with them in their native language of Spanish. As an aside, I share that I returned with 12 fewer pounds of body weight than when I left. That was not my goal as I never weighed myself while I was in Mexico, but I had just before we flew there thinking I would come back having gained weight. That weight loss was a bonus because Mexico taught me so much more than the polishing up of my Spanish skills, it taught me to embrace the "AND", God bless Beautiful Mexico *and* God bless America, the country that I love and will forever be dedicated to. Oh, *and* God bless everywhere else.

The expert in anything was once a beginner.

WHY SABOR? THE PEOPLE, THE MISSION, THE FOOD

"You can take a drug to improve your cholesterol. You can take a drug to reduce your blood pressure. But if you lose weight, you can improve these and the constellation of other metabolic abnormalities because they all track together." – **Samuel Klein, M.D.**
Washington University School of Medicine in St. Louis

The title of this book is separated into two parts and was purely intentional, (1) "Inspire Me, Ms. America" and (2) "A Journey to Wellness con SABOR"; the goal was to evoke curiosity for the prospective reader enough that they would pick it up and investigate why this author is calling herself Ms. America. Notice it is not Miss America but Ms.; First clue. To this point, the entirety of the book has been dedicated to sharing memories and life experiences that have contributed to the name Ms. America and to the memories of my association with food and how it led me to trigger illness in my body.

The pageant song was first sung to me at the young age of 8 years old, mostly as a term of endearment, to remind me of my worth. Looking back, I believe my mother used it at the most stressful times in our lives. It was a coping mechanism, an escape so we both could forget current events that were constantly fragile and unsteady. The origin of the song was during a time in life when television was new, and our society was still very much influenced by our British past. I had a chance to research the very first film clips of these televised Beauty Pageants in America. It was 1954 when this song debuted and my first thought was that the Beauty Queen, after being crowned and dressed in her regalia, while taking her final walk down the runway, crown, scepter, and cape endowed, resembled that worn by Queen Elizabeth at her coronation.

Today, in an effort to adapt to the societal pressures to be "PC", (politically correct), the current pageants are much less about pomp and circumstance, and more about empowering women. In fact, the song to which I am referring is no longer sung and the whole event is popular only in much smaller circles. Nevertheless for me, when she'd say, "Okay Mija, now go down to the end of the hallway and then walk to me when I start singing the Miss America song but walk slowly and don't forget to hold your head up as if you were balancing a book on top." I would immediately stop what I was doing and rush to go look for the tiara made of foil paper, put it on, and wait for Mama to sing. The tiara was very special to me as it was made by me and my Mama as a crafting project on one of those days when she was experiencing a patch of sobriety. Walking down that hall and hearing her sing to me somehow evoked feelings of hope, and escape for those brief seconds. I felt loved and accepted. I felt like everything was going to be alright.

This serves as one of my fondest memories with Mama but I understand now that it was never all about me. As I got older, I understood that revelation more and more. Mama sang it as a "catch-all" act of love during a very delicate time in her life when she had lost her way. And, I was a little girl, with big responsibilities experiencing childhood trauma that mental health specialists now identify as Adverse Childhood Experiences, or ACE. (See Dr. Nadine Burke -Surgeon General). Please understand that I share these familial past dysfunctions and challenges as a guide for the reader and not for pity's sake.

I remember my siblings and I talking about our fathers, there were three fathers in total among the five of us. We talked about how horrible they were to have left a woman who was disabled and had other limitations in life, to care for five children alone. We discussed this using some choice words and ultimately left the conversation upset and angry. That wasn't good for us and only made matters worse.

Since learning about brain health coping methods, I now live with full forgiveness and give grace to all of them, my mother as well as my father, whom I saw in person not more than a handful of times in my life. I believe that parents only know what they know and that parents do the best they can with what life brings them.

Should I have continued to hold a grudge for the stress or sadness that I experienced as a child? I'm sure it would have been easy to do so. However, I'm now aware that the negative emotions associated with that time would have only kept me captive in a mindset of hate, emotions that are not good for the brain. It seems coping takes on many forms, mine was food and sugary foods to be exact.

SUGAR AND THE CRACK FACTORY

Just like Mama had to come to grips with her alcohol addiction, I succumbed to Type 2 Diabetes in my mid-40s because of an addiction of my own, sugar. "Your blood sugar came back indicating that your A1c is now in the Diabetic range and you will have to begin treatment. "Please take this prescription for Metformin and come back to see me in three months," said Dr. Wayne. As many others do, I ignored it. I picked up the script and even took a pill here and there but acted like it was no big deal and continued to eat and drink what I wanted with no regard to the disease. I worked for a food manufacturing company at the time and the main food that was processed involved sugar. Just like alcohol, once consumed regularly, I found that I could NOT live without it and that sugar intake activates the same area of the brain that drugs do. The term sugarholic is a true condition and its definition is someone who is addicted to sugar.

"Sugar is a perfectly legal stimulant drug which releases dopamine in the brain and affects pleasure." **open.ac.uk**

MOVING ON

Eventually, the job's requirements affected my work-life balance and it began to damage my relationship with my family, so I knew it was time to move on.

"The crack addict had to quit the crack dealer", that was step one. After resigning, I immediately felt better because I didn't have the sugar around me to digest daily. Once again, I ignored going back to the doctor for my quarterly check-up. Then our life changed for the better and we moved far away into a beautiful resort community with lots of festivities and food and drink, my kind of life!

Fast forward to a year of living in our new environment. I remember shopping and I started to feel dizzy and super thirsty, even nauseous. Drinking water helped, but I knew I was being irresponsible with my health so I found a new doctor and received the shock of my life. The varying A1c (blood work) levels are as follows, for a non-diabetic 5.5 - 6.0, pre-diabetic 6.1 to 6.8, and a diabetic, that is well controlled, 6.9 -7.0. My blood work showed an A1c of 11.9. Just a few points higher and I would have had to be admitted into the hospital. That's why they call T2D the "silent killer". I was dizzy and thirsty, so what? My body was trying to tell me to take care of it. I learned that my desire to live well on into my senior years has to be stronger than my FOMO, Fear of Missing Out.

As we've already covered SABOR means flavor and while much of the flavor in our fast food industry comes from three addictive substances; salt, fat, and sugar; sugar remains number one on that list. Let's be aware of what we're doing and what we're allowing in our homes, not stick our heads in the sand acting like contracting a life-threatening disease will not happen to us.

If we can go out of our way to recycle plastic, recycle bags, and conserve excess water usage, then we can make eating well and managing our health a priority as well. Does it sound like I'm scolding here? - Sorry, Not Sorry!

SAVE OUR KIDS - (Just a little humor), BUT, just like the saying goes, *Many a truth is said in Jest!*

SUBSTITUTES FOR A HEALTHY DIET:

NOODLES-ZUCCHINI
CHIPS-CARROTS
MILK-COCONUT MILK
RICE-CAULIFLOWER
BUTTER-SADNESS
SUGAR-A BROKEN HEART
CHEESE-NOPE
COFFEE-THIS IS STUPID AND I'M NOT DOING IT

I want to begin a revolution to save our kids and our aging population. Concerned with both ends of the life spectrum, they will be those most vulnerable and at the highest risk for poor quality of life due to medical complications if we allow this trajectory to persist.

OBESITY AND DIABETES

"When I first started my practice, I had never heard of Type 2 Diabetes in children," Says Barry Reiner, M.D. Pediatric Endocrinologist. He continues to say that, "By 2060 the number of people under 20 with Type 2 Diabetes will increase by 700%... As early as 10 -12 years after their childhood diagnosis, patients can start developing nerve damage, kidney problems, and vision damage." *A360 Media* - **The Future of Weight Loss**

HEALTH AND WELLNESS CON SABOR -
FACEBOOK PRIVATE GROUP

Two years ago, I decided that if I was to eventually write this book, I would first have to have some credibility other than my academic degrees and Brain Health License, so I turned to social media, namely FaceBook, which was at its peak. Now, I hear that FB is for mothers, aunties, and grandmothers to keep up with long-distance relatives. Nonetheless, I decided to start a private FB group for those who were interested in supporting one another on their wellness journey. Overall, it's been a hit. Nothing like going viral, well it couldn't because it is a private group, and if you wanted to be included, you'd have to be invited, but I do have a few members shy of one hundred. It was important for me to be inclusive of all those who are following different avenues on their journey to health and wellness. There was no advertising allowed and no cost to join, I only required that the participants would, from time to time, contribute a success story, recipe, comment, or quote that was uplifting and positive regarding health and wellness.

My focus on the word SABOR was two-fold; food has to have flavor, NO CARDBOARD BOX DINNERS ALLOWED, and two, each letter in SABOR had a meaning that supports the FB group's mission and vision. The acronym shares the foundation for the group's vision.

S.A.B.O.R.

(S) Satiety – Food that makes you feel satisfied and full will help keep you on track. That is good fat and lean protein, some fruit, and the addition of spices to foods that need added flavor. A meal that is attractive and tastes unlike "diet" food. Low-carb foods will help in this area as they allow for a slight increase in healthy fat and that will contribute to satiety. In Chapter One, *Eating Like a Gabacho*, we discuss the dilemma of having to choose good food over a healthy lifestyle.

(A) Awareness – Become aware of the food choices in front of you. Literally, go through menu options and say to yourself, I can eat that, but not that. Eventually, the body will crave the foods that you give it. Practice Hada Hachi Foo - learning to stop eating when you feel 80% full, (reference - Live to 100, Secrets of the Blue Zone). In Chapter Five, *Our Thoughts and the Awesome Brain*, we review the power of our thoughts and how being aware of what we are thinking at any given moment can help monitor our reactions to the situation or shift out of one that isn't serving us well.

(B) Believe – Believe that optimal brain health is achievable. Push back the naysayers and flood your mind with stories of people who are achieving the goal you are striving to attain. Stay in that mindset. If you notice that you are wavering, shift out of it by listening to music or taking a walk in the fresh air. In *Ms. America and the White Swan*, the little girl in that story stayed in a positive mindset whether she realized what she was doing or not, and she focused on the people who loved her and helped her to believe in herself.

(O) Organize – Organization equals success, period. The saying goes "90% preparation and 10% execution results in success". The 90% prep takes commitment, discipline, and organization. In Chapter Six, *Mexico Lindo and the Paradox of "AND"* had it not been for that rigorous schedule at the Spanish language institute, they would have never seen the results they did.

(R) Resourcefulness – Finding a way when there seems to be no way. Chapter Two, *La Casa Blanca & Tia Love*. The situation was grim but even clotheslines made of discarded guitar strings made it better. Adopt the "When life gives you lemons, make lemonade mentality". When the forgotten M&M's fell out of the glove compartment in my car on a day when I was "killin' it" with my nutritional eating goals, I simply laughed and said, "Get behind me Satan!" and tossed them into the trash.

Girl, clap for yourself. You've worked hard to get here.

WALK THE TALK

Firecracker, bubbly, and encouraging are just a few of the words I have heard describe my demeanor and personality. I choose inspirational and that has become my business brand. My first book was written in an effort to support teams in the workplace during the recent pandemic of 2020, *A Workforce INSPIRED 2nd Edition, Understanding Diversity, Brain Health, and a Pandemic for Business Sake, 2023.*

Honestly, my continuous improvement mindset doesn't let me rest. Once I've attained one goal, I am constantly looking for a way to strategize for the next. The Facebook page was a good start, but I knew we could do more. We began a YouTube Podcast titled, *A Podcast INSPIRED*. It focuses on subjects that have to do with the four systems of the brain, specifically, mind, body, social, and spirit-related issues.

a podcast

INSPIRED

DOLORES NEIRA

LYRIC NICOLINI

I took up walking as my main exercise and currently, I am up to 85 to 100 miles a month. I requested a CGM, Continuous Glucose Monitor for constant blood sugar level readings. I have also had my meds adjusted and finally, I began to feel better and to feel like I had some control.

I think of myself as one of those blow-up clown punching bags from the 1960's. For those too young to recall, it was about 4 feet tall and had packed down sand at its base to help keep it upright. The goal was to punch it and watch it lay down on the floor from the impact of the punch but eventually, without fail, it would rise again. The purpose was to punch it, get your frustrations out, laugh a little because who likes creepy clowns anyhow, and then try again. Just when you thought he was down… it would come up again. The grin on its face was instigative. The only REAL way you could get that clown to stay down was to pop it!

As I have written about in previous chapters, Type 2 Diabetes can be managed. Once you know that you have the disease, immediately incorporate the following priorities into your life.

1. **Become an expert.** Bring a journal of notes and questions to your doctor's visit. Do some pre-work, so that you can get the most out of the meeting. Take notes of what was said and what needs to be done and repeat what you wrote and learned before leaving the appointment. Spiral notebooks worked well for me and the cost was minimal, one dollar.

2. **Plan everything.** Plan your meals, plan your activities, plan your meds, and understand why you're taking the drugs that have been prescribed.

3. **Find the median.** It's not "all" or "nothing", find the middle ground for life's situations. Sometimes we need to give ourselves grace and allow for some days where we just don't know.

4. **Be Assertive!** Not aggressive or passive but assertive as if your life depended on it, because, honestly, it does. If you don't understand something, ask! It's not rude to ask for clarification. As I train in many of my workshops, it's not asking for something to be clarified that is the issue, but *how* you ask for the clarification. Use something like this; "Excuse me but I do not understand those terms you just used to describe my condition, can you please clarify?"

5. **Talk to your pharmacist.** They want to be proactive and help, it is much better to ask up front than to clean up a mess after a mix-up in meds has occurred.

Overall, come to grips that if you have the disease, admit it and begin working on reversing it, (Type 2 Diabetes only). If you are a pre-diabetic or have children who are going down that road, do everything in your power to sit down and share your concerns then move into action. Never mind what the Naysayers say, just do it now!

> **More protein**
> **More fat**
> **More movement**
> **More rest**
> **More listening to music**
> **More sunlight**
> **More walks**
> **More purpose**
> **More creativity**
> **More time with friends/family**

Blessings <3

eight

"HELLO, NINE TOES?" THIS IS WAR!

"You're Ripping them off by playing soft." **– Loral Langemeier**

On my way to a 50th Anniversary Gala event for a non-profit organization of a business client, I wondered what the dinner meal would consist of and if they would be serving something semi-healthy. This type of preparation has become common practice for me these days and is one of my methods to manage my Type 2 Diabetes. As we covered in Chapter Seven, SABOR is an acronym and the "O" stands for organization, specifically, preparation. The event was planned for many years before this evening so once again, I see evidence that 90% preparation and 10% execution made all the difference, it was amazing. The meal was "delish", complete with options of grilled chicken, fish, beef or vegetarian meals, and two servings of vegetables with minimal carbohydrates. New potatoes grilled in garlic butter were a perfect addition of "good carbs".

As the dance portion of the evening began, the live band was playing all the favorites including a few Cumbias, (a Latin American dance similar to Salsa style), songs. We were able to get in a couple dances before sitting down again at our assigned table. I make it a point to keep my phone on silent when I am at social events because I try to stay present and in the moment. It just so happens that as I was searching for an after dinner mint in my purse, I noticed the phone light up. By the time I grabbed it, the phone call had ended. I noticed that it was a missed call from one of my nieces. She was the daughter of my brother and we had not kept in contact much lately, so immediately I became concerned. I decided to step out of the event and try to connect with her. Unsuccessful, I went back in and decided to keep my phone near my side. Minutes later, I got a text from my brother. "Just want you to know that we're getting together at Santa Clara Hospital in the morning to pray for our brother, he will be having his toes amputated. If you are nearby, please come and gather with us, sorry for the short notice, he just let us know" We lived four hours from that hospital and it was 9:30pm when we were kicking up our heels in celebration. My husband could see my face just drop. I passed him the phone to read the message for himself. He then asked, "Do you want to leave now?" I motioned with my head, yes.

What occurred next was a whirl wind for me. We hurried back to our hotel and got our suitcase packed and jumped in the car to drive most of the night. Then stopped at another brother's house for a quick nap before heading over to the hospital.

If you've read in order to this point in the book, then you know that we, (my siblings and I), were all raised to be very independent. If nothing else, our early days as a family under one roof taught us to take care of ourselves. Granted, we were there for each other should they need us, but hardships were something we just knew how to handle, so we kept them private. Don't misunderstand, when we did get the opportunity to get together, it was surely a grand party! Four of the five of us are loud or jokesters or both! We do a lot of laughing and reminiscing about our past and one of us has to put on some type of theater about someone else's demeanor.

As families often do, we hadn't made it a priority to get a date down on the calendar for the next family "get-together", so I really didn't know too much about my siblings' personal life. You see, I left Santa Clara County to go away to college when I was just 18 years young. The first in my family, I mean my ENTIRE family, all 50 plus relatives, in my generational line and before me, to step foot on a college campus. I spoke of this in Chapter Two, La Casa Blanca & Sister Love. As we are all aware, life goes on and some of us move away from the family nucleus while knowing that there is a risk to potentially grow apart. Is there guilt, absolutely, so I think that the feeling of guilt was what came over me more than anything in that moment.

We got to the hospital in time and we found him lying unconscious on the bed in his hospital room getting ready to be taken into surgery. His purple toes on his left foot were exposed and a couple were looking darker than the others, almost to the point that they were gray-black in color. That's when I had a flash-back from my childhood. I remembered the tips of my mother's finger on her "bum arm"(her words not mine), being the same color. I decided, then and there, not to think too much about the current situation and instead just pray in my spirit, meaning under my breath.

We were told by the nurse that the doctor was ready for my brother and to return later that evening after he was out of recovery. We stepped back as they rolled him out of his hospital room and all I could think was, "I'm sorry that I wasn't here for you Bro" as tears were running down my face. If you read La Casa Blanca, you'll recall that early on in my young life, I was responsible for my brother's well being, when my mother wasn't able to function well. Even to the point that they would joke about that time and refer to me as "Cinderella". The following poem came to mind, just as I silently shared my apologies with my brother.

READY FOR THE CLIMB

You can't carry people when you're trying to get to the top, it will slow you down. But there's survivor remorse that comes with it. For those who got the opportunity to go to college away from home and left their family, knowing that they are struggling to eat back home and you are deciding if you will use your student loan money to send back home so that your mama can pay the electric bill instead of buying your books for class. If you want to make it you will have to make some hard choices about what to do. For the people who came along with you and they couldn't make it, you will have to leave them behind and keep climbing and when you make it to the top, you'll be able to reach back and help them. It is one of the greatest challenges you'll ever have when you are pursuing a life that is drastically different from the life you came from.

Former First Lady Michelle Obama speaking on the dilemma of first-generation college students. (Instagram: Gratitudegalaxie)

I PIVOT AND SAY NO MAS!

So what if you have…

» A beautiful new car, but you can't drive it because you have limited ability to use your feet due to uncontrolled, T2D?

» An amazing family, if you are not going to see them graduate college or get married?

» A college degree from the most prestigious educational institution if you won't be able to share that knowledge with those who need you to help pull them up?

» A lottery win, in the millions, if you won't ever be able to spend or share it?

I don't want to "rip you off by playing soft" because the harsh reality is, we are losing this war! We're getting sicker! Our children potentially have a future that is drastically different from ours. Fifty percent will be sicker sooner in their lifetimes than ever before in the history of the USA.

Well I say "NO MAS!" No more! And just like my Tia Delia did when she entered a machine factory, unprepared and as a novice only to became one of the iconic Rosie the Riveters in an effort to support the War, of the 1940s, I am destined to do what I can to turn around these horrendous statistics for T2D cases that are on the rise in our county. Why? Mahatma Gandhi said that we need to "Be the change that you want to see", and that starts with me.

"THE OBJECTIVE IS NOT WEIGHT LOSS, BUT HEALTH GAIN!"

We have this thing all wrong. Here's how the outside world is affecting our health. Our modern era is proposing many unhealthy influences that push us into a cycle of obesity.

» Increased availability of energy-dense, nutrition-poor foods and beverages. Chips, sodas, even energy drinks with high sugar added.

» Pervasive food advertising - I counted 23 commercials for pizza and hamburgers in a 2 hour span of late night shows on cable TV. I wasn't feeling hungry when I started out, and by the end of that show, I wanted a burger really badly.

» Larger portion sizes - You really aren't getting a deal for those sizes in the long run.

» Environmental and chemical toxins.

» Revolving door diets, which lead to weight cycling - aka yo-yo dieting

» Maternal overnutrition during pregnancy

» Lack of health care provider support and knowledge about wellness

» Labor saving devices that increase sedentary lifestyles - DoorDash.

I know that we still have the freedom to choose, however the food industry wants to fool us and fool us they have!

The problem with our industrial food system

99¢ $5

I returned to the hospital as soon as they mentioned I was able to and asked for directions to see my brother. He was in another hospital room and unconscious once again,what I saw next was like being transported into the HBO war special Band of Brothers. I walked in,looked down and saw what I thought to be half of his foot gone! I recall immediately feeling nauseated and wanting to vomit. It wasn't like I was not fully aware of what was going to happen but when it actually did, it was surreal. It truly was like he was in a scene in a war medical hospital.

Looking for some moral support, I reached out to another childhood friend that lived close to the hospital and left her several messages letting her know what was going on with my brother. She and I have been friends since elementary school and our relationship was similar to that of Chill and mine. After several attempts to contact her, she hadn't contacted me back. I wondered to myself, that was strange, she was usually pretty quick at responding.

Still in the hospital room waiting for my brother to wake up, I finally received a text from her instructing me to call her when I had a minute because the text was too personal and would be too long to share on the phone. Time went by and my brother finally opened his eyes, glanced around and then looked down to his feet and began to weep. His other family members were there as well, so I left them to have their privacy and went out to call my friend.

"Hey girl, where have you been? I'm at the hospital near your house." I asked. She responded by saying, "I'm at the same hospital with my dad, on the fourth floor." I quickly asked why and she responded, "I have been here for the past few days because he's been really sick and almost died." She went on to say, "I don't remember telling you but he has Type 2 Diabetes and when I found him he was in pretty bad shape." What she said next sent me to my knees on the floor. She continued in a sobbing voice, "He only told us of his complications after he was in severe pain and because of that the doctors couldn't do much about it, so they just had to amputate his leg." Why didn't someone tell us? Why haven't they put out an urgent cry for help? This is now an epidemic!

While writing this book, what I have learned more than anything else is that I/we have to learn for ourselves. We have to make the effort to ask questions, do research, and read what we can about the new advances in Diabetic disease management. At present, my family is all on their respective journeys for optimal health and wellness. We share ideas and cheer for each other after a good blood work report. There is no shaming, or condemnation, just open and honest communication around mental health and wellness which include managing our Type 2 Diabetes.

My brothers are still the "Malcriados" that I spoke about in chapter six. You would think that once they entered their 60's that behavior would have been washed out. No,they are still acting up and when they talk with each other over the phone, you can hear them asking, "Hello, is this Nine Toes?" Funny but not funny, although they still get a good laugh.

In contrast, when I call them by phone it is certain that you'll hear me say, "Hey Bro, how are you doing and so, what's your A1c looking like?"

Mine went from A1(c) 11.9 when I first found out about my diagnoses of being Diabetic to an A1 (c) 6.8 within a year. I continue to monitor this number every three to six months. This journey of learning how to handle a new lifestyle is constant and I am strategizing my preventative tactics because I intend to win this war.

"You don't need to be perfect to inspire others. Let people get inspired by how you deal with your imperfection."

Exercise!! Your Brain will Thank You!

https://www.facebook.com/watch/?v=10160545401360652

THE HISTORY OF BRAIN DEVELOPMENT

Throughout history, the brain was the only organ in the body that was commonly diagnosed yet never seen. Dr. Amen is most known for creating a brain imaging tool that could identify blood flow in the brain. SPECT scan or Single Photon Emission Computed Tomography. Follow the SIX to FIX.

https://www.facebook.com/watch/?v=859632301849154

"You Can Change Your Life by Changing Your Brain"
Dr. Daniel Amen, MD

The best medicine by far = whole foods made at home and shared with the family.

Be kind to one another *"You never know how much someone is carrying because they may be carrying it well."*

DEDICATION

This book is dedicated to my readers. Those of you who have picked up this book, in curiosity, and committed to reading it, really reading it. My hopes are that you are impacted by the stories and statistics shared within these pages and that it has inspired you to adopt and embrace a new way of life.

Shame is not necessary for change, however, acting on your desire to live well is.

Seek help, don't betray who you were really meant to be. Please put your health as #1- first on your priority list.

Blessings <3

I welcome you to find me. For more information,

www.poandassociates.com

WORKS CITED

Amen, Daniel G. *Change Your Brain Every Day: Simple Daily Practices to Strengthen Your Mind, Memory, Moods, Focus, Energy, Habits, and Relationships.* Christian Art Publishers, 2023.

Amen, Daniel G. *Change Your Brain, Change Your Life.* Piatus, 2016.

Amen, Daniel G. *The End of Mental Illness How Neuroscience Is Transforming Psychiatry and Helping Prevent or Reverse Mood and Anxiety Disorders, ADHD, Addictions, PTSD, Psychosis, Personality.* Tyndale House Pub, 2024.

Amen, Daniel G. *You, Happier.* TYNDALE HOUSE PUBLISHERS, 2022.

Amen, Daniel G. *Your Brain Is Always Listening: Tame the Hidden Dragons That Control Your Happiness, Habits,... and Hang-Ups.* TYNDALE REFRESH, 2022.

Brown, Brené. *Atlas of the Heart Mapping Meaningful Connection and the Language of Human Experience.* Ebury Digital, 2022.

Fisch, Jen. *The Easy 5-Ingredient Ketogenic Diet Cookbook: Low-Carb, High-Fat Recipes for Busy People on the Keto Diet.* Rockridge Press, 2018.

Hyman, Mark. *The Blood Sugar Solution Cookbook: More than 175 Ultra-Tasty Recipes for Total Health and Weight Loss.* Little, Brown and Company, 2013.

Leaf, Caroline. *Cleaning up Your Mental Mess: 5 Simple, Scientifically Proven Steps to Reduce Anxiety, Stress, and Toxic Thinking.* Baker Books, a Division of Baker Publishing Group, 2021.

Maslow, Abraham H., et al. *Maslow on Management.* John H. Wiley & Sons, 2000.

Pick, Marcelle. *Is It Me or My Hormones?* Hay House UK Ltd, 2013. *Secrets for Beating Diabetes: Simple, Everyday Tips to Transform Your Health.* Reader's Digest Association, 2017.

What to Eat Now. Wiley, 2011.

RECIPES

Please scan this QR code with your phone
for the recipes.

TESTIMONIALS

Mrs. Dolores Neira! I met this lovely lady through her husband. My first encounter was instant admiration for her. She is a born teacher! Always searching for knowledge and paying it forward. Her love for life and people comes to her naturally. She is a person who always sees the glass half full and tells you why! I have enjoyed her health, fitness, recipes, and life lesson advice.
Con Amor y Sabor Keep on truckin' Lola!

- Vivian Bell

Dolores has put her heart and soul into investigating how brain health and wellness options can help those struggling with Type 2 Diabetes. Since 2022, when she first became a Licensed Brain Health Trainer with Amen Clinics, she has impressed me with her willingness and passion to share this information with not only her business clients but her family and friends. I look forward to May 2024, when I can read a copy of her new book, Inspire Me, Ms. America! A Journey to Wellness con SABOR!

- Barbara Gustavson, Head Facilitator for
Dr. Amen's Professional Certification Courses

"I have followed SABOR, this health group that beautifully integrates Mexican culture into its message since its inception. Not only does it offer delicious and nutritious recipes, but it also celebrates the vibrant flavors and ingredients of Mexican cuisine. Each recipe is a delightful fusion of health-conscious choices and traditional Mexican dishes, making it a feast for both the body and the soul. Whether you're a health enthusiast, a foodie, or someone who simply appreciates good food with a cultural twist, SABOR is a must-visit. ¡Buen provecho!"

- Jessica Rangel

Dolores Neira, MA Education

INSPIRE PERFORMANCE; EXPECT RESULTS.

As the founder of Performance Outcomes & Associates, (POA), Dolores has been positively impacting diverse corporate cultures since 2001. These teams include businesses from non-profits, Education, Manufacturing, Medical, and Agriculture. Dolores is passionate about coaching leaders to adopt a solutions-based, continuous improvement mind-set. She is a Published Author of A Workplace INSPIRED, a Licensed Brain Health Trainer with Dr. Daniel Amen, M.D., and holds a master's in Educational Administration. She is certified in Lean Organizational Development and believes that happy teams are productive teams. Dolores supports giving back to the community and leads many fundraising efforts with various non-profit charitable organizations within her community. She is married to Delfino, her husband of 40 years, and together they have raised three adult children.

Made in the USA
Middletown, DE
01 November 2024

63219582R00082